UNSTOPPABLE
INFLUENCE

Be You. Be Fearless. Transform Lives.

By
Natasha Hazlett

Soul Food
PUBLISHING

For my husband, Rich
Your wisdom, love and unwaivering
support allowed me to find my Truth.
I am blessed to have you by my side.

GRAB YOUR FREE GIFT!

Download the Companion Workbook

(Retails for $39.95…Yours FREE!)

Do you want to get a head start on unleashing your influence in the world? Of *course* you do. You're an Unstoppable Influencer!

You should download the workbook for this edition right now, so you can work along as you read. To access your gift:

1. Go to UnstoppableInfluence.com/Gift.
2. Tell us where to email the access link.
3. Check your email, then download the PDF.
4. Have fun following along as you read the book.

PRAISE FOR
UNSTOPPABLE INFLUENCE

In *Expert Secrets*, I teach the strategy and technology behind building an expert business. But before you can shine your light to the world, you have to know where the switch is. You have to know what you were put on this earth to do, and you have to give yourself permission to share it far and wide.

Natasha Hazlett is the real deal. She has helped thousands of entrepreneurs overcome their fears and build expert businesses that help change lives.

Her book *Unstoppable Influence* gives you the tools to uncover your true purpose and unapologetically share your gifts with the world. If you know you're meant for something greater, get this book!

—Russell Brunson
Co-Founder of ClickFunnels
Best-Selling Author of *Expert Secrets* and *DotComSecrets*

Unstoppable Influence gives us an entertaining, poignant "behind the curtain" look at the journey of a true influencer.

As you read the book, you will understand we do not have to be perfect, self doubt is natural, and designing the life you want is possible.

Natasha writes in a conversational way that gives your the impression she is whispering in your ear and encouraging you every step of the way.

— Patricia Fripp,
Author, *Get What You Want*
Former President, National Speakers Association

"*Unstoppable Influence* is NOT just a book; it's your step-by-step blueprint that will supercharge you to success. Natasha leaves no stone unturned, giving you deep wisdom and sequential action steps that will unleash Unstoppable Influence in all you do."

— Joseph Clough,
Best-Selling Hay House Author
and Celebrity Hypnotherapist

CONTENTS

Part II: Transform Lives
The Roadmap to Unstoppable Influence

FOREWORD

Every so often, a book comes along that makes a difference. This is one of them.

Natasha Hazlett demonstrates the courage to bare her soul and tell her story, warts and all, and gives her readers the inspiration to take the next step. I've read hundreds of self-help books and have found that when one really resonates with you, causes you to fine-tune your belief system, change key behaviors, and take new courses of action, it's worth its weight in gold. It's only through such learning experiences that we change and progress into the next realm of our lives. *Unstoppable Influence* will provide the rocket fuel to propel every cover-to cover reader into the reality of their dreams.

So many people are waiting until everything is perfectly in place to make a major move in their lives. Here's how Natasha suggests you deal with that potentially crippling mental ball and chain.

> You won't always have the answers. But guess what? You don't *need* all the answers. Your desire to have all the answers before taking a step has caused your feet to be cemented

inside your comfort zone, and that's dimming your light!

That's one of hundreds of concepts that prove that her insights belie her years. I've had the pleasure of knowing Natasha and her family for decades, and to follow the exciting path of her growth is truly exhilarating. She learned early on that there are no unrealistic goals—only unrealistic time frames—and that you never lose until you give up! She has shown that if you are determined to exert the effort, you can make the decision to reach up and grab the rest of your destiny.

This is not just a feel-good book. It offers some deep psychological principles that can rock your existence and cause you to take a closer look at why you have behaved the way you have up to this juncture in your life. This is the type of work that challenges you, in a good way, to trash the barriers that have held you back, in deference to immediate action and solid results!

Her perspective on rejection, defeat, and seemingly insurmountable problems demonstrates the value of having the courage to take the next step for personal success. It is no surprise that she has created a tremendous following in her space, which will undoubtedly result in thousands monumentally progressing in their chosen endeavors.

Members of the intelligentsia tell us that humans typically function on only 16% to 18% of their brainpower. This book has a good possibility of jerking its readers out of their complacency and thrusting them into the next level of their existence. It will help you be your best. I plan to read this book once a year well into the future as I continue my journey to a life of betterment. It contains enough gems to keep me going for long while. I think it will for you as well!

Don Hutson,
New York Times and *Wall Street Journal*
#1 Best-Selling Co-Author of *The One Minute Entrepreneur*,
Hall of Fame Speaker, and
CEO of U.S. Learning

I know for sure: Your journey begins with a choice to get up, step out, and live fully

~ Oprah Winfrey

INTRODUCTION

If you want to achieve greatness,
stop asking for permission.

~ Anonymous

For years, people have urged me to write a book. So I started writing one. But a third of the way into the process, something didn't feel quite right. So I shelved it for two years.

However, something the motivational speaker Les Brown said at a seminar I attended nagged at me throughout those two years.

> Imagine, if you will, being on your deathbed. And standing around your bed are the ghosts of the ideas, the dreams, the abilities, the talents given to you by life.
>
> And that you—for whatever reason—you never acted on those ideas, you never pursued that dream, you never used those talents, we never saw your leadership, you never used your voice, you never wrote that book.
>
> And there they are, standing around your bed looking at you with large, angry eyes, saying, "We came to you, and only you could

have given us life! Now we must die with you forever."

The question is: If you died today, what ideas, what dreams, what abilities, what talents, what gifts would die with you? [1]

I didn't want *my* message to die, so here I am finally writing my book.

The title just came to me in a business meeting with my husband/business partner/best friend, Rich. Just as we were getting started, I told him that the uncertainty of where we would live (staying in Boise or moving back down south) was causing me tremendous anxiety, and that we needed to make a decision on that first, *then* talk business.

He agreed.

Within 30 minutes, we'd made our decision.

Next on the agenda was the name of our new brand. For over a year, I knew we needed to retire our *Branded: 100% Authentic* program in order to create something with a broader impact. Yet no matter how hard I tried, I just couldn't figure out the new brand or message.

Over the years, we've learned a lot about a variety of topics, including personal development, business, marketing, branding, copywriting, and strategic planning. Which of these topics were we supposed to share?

As if by magic, within 15 minutes of *finally* deciding where we wanted to live, the phrase Unstoppable Influence popped into my mind.

Rich and I both instantly fell in love with it. Of course, being internet-marketing experts, we immediately hopped on to the computer to see if UnstoppableInfluence.com was taken. To our pleasant surprise, it was available.

In that moment, I knew that Unstoppable Influence would become a movement that would transform lives across the globe.

Next, I googled "unstoppable influence" to check for other brands using the same phrase. The only results that popped up were sermons.

Wow, I thought, *this has a spiritual connection, too!*

Although I don't consider myself to be extremely religious, I'm very spiritual. Creating a movement grounded in applied spiritual principles was exhilarating but scary. So to make sure we were on the right path, I prayed for God to give us confirmation.

After doing some market research, our next step was to hire a graphic designer to create a logo for our movement. After getting concepts from over 20 designers, we noticed one recurring theme—the infinity symbol.

I'd never thought of that symbol before, but when I saw it, I knew it was the perfect fit. Nothing says Unstoppable like an infinity loop—a symbol with no beginning and no end that represents eternity, empowerment, and everlasting love.

As I stared at the symbol, this verse popped into my head: "I am the Alpha and the Omega, the beginning and the ending". [2] It was further confirmation that we were on the right path with our message.

As we shared our new concept with our clients and business mastermind group, they fell in love with the Unstoppable Influence message too.

A few weeks later, two of our mentors, Don Hutson and Terri Murphy, again began strongly encouraging me to write my book. When a colleague invited me to join her program for writing a non-fiction book, it was the final nudge I needed to quit screwing around and just write.

There was just one teeny, tiny problem—I didn't have a damn clue what to write about! Seriously.

You may think I'm exaggerating, but there's a reason I hadn't written a book yet. I may have plenty to say on stage, on the phone, in a Facebook Live, or in my training programs, but when it comes to writing a book that's 50,000 words long, that's a little (ahem) intimidating.

Plus, I wanted to write a *New York Times* Best Seller straight out of the gate, one that would transform millions of lives. If my book didn't hit the best-seller list, as far as I was concerned, it wasn't worth writing.

In hindsight, I was being *totally* selfish. By putting such a ridiculous amount of pressure on myself, I managed to avoid writing a book for 13…freaking…years. That genius plan had resulted in the transformation of a grand total of *zero* lives. Pitiful. It was time to get over myself and just write the darn book.

That wasn't the only hurdle I faced, though.

One of my biggest fears was the sheer magnitude of the Unstoppable Influence movement. Its importance weighed heavily on me. I felt like I needed to say the *right* things the *right* way, because people I didn't even know yet were counting on me to give them the exact roadmap to Unstoppable Influence. So it took me nearly a month to even schedule the first few days of writing.

Ultimately, I decided to release my fears and let God lead me through the process. As the first day of book writing approached, I decided that instead of mapping out the entire book, I would simply turn off my internet and phone, open up a blank Word document, and just type whatever came to me.

I promised myself I would resist the urge to go back and edit. Instead, I would just "wing it." Sounds crazy, I know. Yet for some strange reason, this plan helped release all my anxiety about writing this book.

So on Day 1, I walked into the office, prayed, did a few short breathing exercises, dabbed on a few essential oils, turned up some Ryan Farish tunes, and opened my computer.

As the blank document stared back at me, I closed my eyes and started typing. I felt inspired. I was "in-Spirit" as Dr. Wayne Dyer dubbed it in his book, *Living an Inspired Life*. I was tapping into my Truth and, as a result, the words flowed freely onto the page.

The next day, I resisted the temptation to read what I had typed the day before. I followed my routine: prayer, breathing exercises, essential oil, and Ryan Farish. The words continued to flow.

At this point, some of y'all may be freaked out that I'm using the G-word (God). Heads up—I might mix things up and use the words Spirit, Source, or Creator as well.

Here's my legal disclaimer of sorts, one that I saw on a coffee cup, no less!

I love Jesus, but I swear a little!

If that bothers you, go ahead and slip this book back onto the shelf and walk away. But if you're okay with a little spicy language, then keep on reading, friend!

I should also mention that in addition to swearing on occasion, I also like to drink wine…and I'm a Christian. Truth be told, I'm more spiritual than religious. I regularly attend church, but my focus is on developing my relationship with God, not following man-made rules. That said, I refuse to judge others for their beliefs or lack thereof.

At the end of the day, most of us can agree on one basic concept—there's a Source of energy and light through which all life is created. So it doesn't matter if you think God is a man, a woman, or a zebra. Words are just words. So feel free to substitute your word of choice for God—Universe, Source, Grand Poobah, or even Zebra.

Ultimately, it's the underlying message that's important. It's the message that you're here *on* purpose and *for* a purpose. If you're reading this book right now, you're an Unstoppable Influencer at your core—you just might not know it yet.

This book will help you to finally tap into your potential and unleash your influence in the world so that you can fulfill your life's purpose. If that sounds awesome, then buckle up, turn the page, and let's get started!

PART I

BE YOU. BE FEARLESS.

Once you become fearless, life becomes limitless.

Unknown

CHAPTER 1

WHAT IS UNSTOPPABLE INFLUENCE?

This little light of mine, I'm going to let it shine.
Let it shine! Let it shine! Let it shine!
Ev'ry where I go, I'm going to let it shine!
Oh, ev'ry where I go, I'm going to let it shine!

~ Harry Dixon Loes, "This Little Light of Mine"

Just like it says in the gospel song "This Little Light of Mine," which I learned as a child in Sunday school, I believe you're called to share your light with the world. When you're given a gift, it's your duty to share it with others because it makes the world a brighter place.

Every year at the end of the Christmas Eve service, our church goes completely dark as the choir sings "Silent Night." The pastor takes the flame from his own candle and shares it with a few people. That group then takes their candles to the front row and they share their flames with others. One by one, each person uses their own flame to light their neighbor's candle.

Within minutes, the entire church is filled with a radiant glow as the entire congregation sings "Silent Night."

You're the candle, my friend. When you were born, God ignited your flame—it's your gift. Your flame wasn't meant to be kept in a box. The purpose of your gift is to share it with others.

As an Unstoppable Influencer, you're the keeper of a precious flame. You can't allow your flame to dim, because then others won't be able to use it to brighten their *own* candles. Of course, life will throw you curve balls; they'll put your flame in jeopardy if you're not careful. That's why you must *learn* to become Unstoppable.

You see, being Unstoppable isn't something you're born with—it's a *skill* that must be mastered. But how?

By equipping yourself with the tools necessary to keep your flame glowing brightly amid adversity, self-doubt, fear, and any other negative force that tries to diminish it.

You can resist those negative forces and keep your flame glowing. And that, my friend, is what this book is all about. You'll get the clarity, confidence, and strategies you need to become the Unstoppable Influencer you were born to be.

Because you are reading this, I believe you've been tapped as an Influencer. I don't think that everyone is called to be one, but you've been. That said, you must do the work necessary to master not only becoming Unstoppable, but also the strategies necessary to unleash your gifts and influence in the world.

Now you may be thinking, "Natasha, surely you're not calling ME an Influencer. If you knew anything about me, you wouldn't be saying that!"

Yes, I would.

I've written this book for one reason and one reason only. To provide Influencers with the tools they need to become Unstoppable and make the biggest possible impact in the world with their gifts.

I'm confident that the title of this book will attract the right people. So if you're reading this, congratulations! You're on your way to becoming an Unstoppable Influencer. There are several important concepts you need to know about this role.

First, you're NOT immune from pain, disappointment, fear, anxiety, or a lack of self-confidence. Some of the most influential people I know have endured tremendous physical, emotional, and mental trauma. Influencers are *perfectly imperfect*, and that's how it's supposed to be.

You must acknowledge the pain and struggle and learn *how* to use these experiences gifted to you by life in a way that spreads more light in the world.

Secondly, realize that Influencers don't have to have it *all* figured out. You're a work in progress, just like I am. For example, as I type this chapter, I don't have this entire book figured out. Can you believe it?

I don't have a chapter list or outline. In fact, I have no idea how it'll all unfold. I just know that I'm supposed to write this book. So here I sit, completely open to the inspiration gifted to me so that I can share it with you. I hope that you too will be open as you continue reading.

5

Finally, it doesn't matter how many followers you have on Facebook or Instagram, Twitter or Pinterest. That's superficial nonsense that has no bearing on your ability to become an Unstoppable Influencer. So don't worry about that at all.

There may be some concepts in this book that you don't understand, or that you disagree with. That's okay! Take what resonates with you and discard the rest. You don't need to agree with everything to still learn a whole lot.

Also know that the journey to becoming an Unstoppable Influencer is distinct to *you*. As you read the chapters that follow, I encourage you to pray or meditate on them.

Download your copy of the *Companion Workbook* for FREE at UnstoppableInfluence.com/gift so you can record your ideas and complete exercises that will help you apply the concepts I teach to your own life. These bits of inspiration will be helpful as you move forward on your path to Unstoppable Influence.

LET'S REVIEW

- ❖ You were created *on* purpose and *for* a purpose. You're called to share your light (and gifts) with the world.
- ❖ Even those who are called to be Influencers must master the skill of becoming Unstoppable.
- ❖ Influencers are NOT immune from pain, disappointment, fear, anxiety, or lack of self-confidence. In fact, you typically must experience these emotions as part of your journey.

❖ You don't need to have everything figured out. You'll learn along the way.

❖ It doesn't matter how many followers you have on Facebook or Instagram, Twitter or Pinterest. That has no bearing on your mission as an Unstoppable Influencer.

❖ Be open to the inspiration being gifted to you.

TAKE ACTION NOW

1. Commit to reading this book in its entirety, so that you're fully equipped to unleash your influence in the world. Better yet, set a deadline for reading this book or target dates for reading one chapter at a time.

2. Be OPEN. Meditate or pray on concepts you don't understand or that you disagree with. Allow yourself to entertain new concepts, even if they don't align perfectly with your current belief system. As Aristotle once said, "It is the mark of an educated mind to be able to entertain a thought without accepting it."

3. Download your copy of the *Unstoppable Influence Companion Workbook* for FREE at UnstoppableInfluence.com/gift so you can record your inspiration and access additional tools and resources for the journey ahead.

CHAPTER 2

LIVING A LIFE BY DESIGN, NOT DEFAULT

*You only live once, but if you do it right,
once is enough.*

~ Mae West

The concept of living life by design has captured my attention for years. Although it wasn't until years after I first heard it that I understood its *true* meaning.

I *thought* it meant having the ability to work where you want, when you want, and with whoever you want, while getting paid well. I believed this concept to my core, so I shared it with others as a goal we should all strive for.

As internet entrepreneurs, Rich and I can travel the world 24/7 and conduct business from our laptops. We enjoy going on impromptu trips, traveling through Europe for three weeks, and visiting our family for nearly a month, never once having to ask a boss for time off.

I thought we were living life by design, and it was awesome! I wanted to show people how to create and run an online business so they too could live life by design. However, a couple years later, I discovered that life by design is far more pro-found than that.

It all became clear when I was asked to speak at the Memphis Women's Summit.

The plan was for me to teach the audience how to live their lives by design. I wanted to open their minds to online opportunities to monetize their talents and gifts, so they too could work where they wanted, when they wanted, with people they enjoyed serving, and make *way* more money than at a "regular" j-o-b.

However, as I started writing my speech, the subject matter took a detour. As a woman of faith, I recognize moments where I'm being led by the Spirit. As I wrote my talk, I discovered that this was one of those moments.

So I continued typing, reserving judgment until after all the words were on the page. Several hours later, as I reread my 17-page speech, I thought, "Hot damn! Look at this masterpiece!"

I'd somehow successfully woven my story and the lessons I'd learned over the past decade into one profound speech that I knew would change lives.

There was just one tiny problem. Sharing these sorts of lessons was *way* outside my comfort zone. I'd never spoken about spirituality or personal development, and I wasn't sure I could do so with any level of authority.

But as I read and reread the words in front of me, I couldn't deny their truth. *This* was my Truth.

As I delivered my talk to four separate audiences, I saw everything from tears welling up to heads vigorously nodding. I watched as people experienced life-changing epiphanies before me.

Every time I exited the stage, I was greeted with hugs and personal stories that gave me the validation I sought—I had found my message and delivered it just as God had intended.

My parents sat in one of the audiences. I watched their expressions change as they began to finally understand who I really was and what motivated me to make unconventional decisions like leaving my family and friends down south to move to Boise, Idaho, where I knew no one.

My dad walked up to me afterward and said, "I learned a lot about you that I never knew. I'm proud of you."

I was finally operating in my Zone of Truth, and it showed. The audience, and especially my parents, felt it. Ironically, *this* was the moment when I truly began living my life by design.

I've said it before, and I'll say it throughout this book because it's *that* important: You're here *on* purpose and *for* a purpose.

You were made in the perfect image of your Creator, and your life has meaning. Living life by design isn't about sipping piña coladas in Tahiti every day; it's about living in alignment with your Truth and purpose in life. When your Creator gave you life, He blessed you with gifts that only *you* can share with the world. You're one of a kind, don't forget it!

In living life by design, you'll uncover these gifts and fulfill your calling as an Unstoppable Influencer who *unleashes* your message in the world for the betterment of all. You'll leave a legacy that ultimately makes the world a better place, because you've made an indelible mark.

The great news is that living life by design isn't rocket science. You were already designed in the image of your Creator. You have everything you need within you *right now*. It just takes a little practice and reawakening to your Truth. Let's start the process, shall we?

LIVING YOUR LIFE BY DESIGN

Most people spend their lives in a state of default. Their habits and daily routines run deep, like ruts in a field.

You move along the same track every day. You drive the same way to work, shop at the same grocery store, pay the same bills, go to sleep at the same time. Wake up and do it all over again.

The more you follow the same ol' same ol', the deeper the ruts get. Before you know it, you no longer have to steer your life—it just follows the track.

If you've ever driven in ruts, you know that as long as you stay in the track, it's smooth sailing. The car will practically drive itself.

But if you try to deviate from the track, depending on how deep the rut is, all hell could break loose! Your tires may spin out of control. You may pop a tire or, if you're particularly unfortunate, your car may get stuck.

You'll face similar challenges when attempting to get yourself out of one of life's ruts. It's difficult and sometimes painful.

Frequently, as you meet some resistance, you give up and go back to running on the old tracks because, well, it's easier that way.

When you're living life by default, you're uninspired, bored, and unfulfilled. The reason? You're disconnected from your Source (God). When that happens, you miss out on the inspiration and information you need to live in alignment with your purpose.

Here's the thing—just because everyone else is in a rut doesn't mean you need to be too. It's *abnormal* to live out of alignment with your purpose, because it's contrary to how you were designed!

So how *do* you get out of the rut of living life by default?

The first step is to recognize your own gifts. If you're not sure what they are, then commit to uncovering them. You'll need to connect with God on this one—and be open to the resources and tools you're given to help you in the process.

Next, you must be courageous and bold enough to say "Hell yeah!" to your life's purpose, and share your gift with the world. Then commit to growing into the best damn version of yourself, so that you can fulfill your calling.

TRUTH TIME

I can't say that I've always lived my life by design—not by a long shot. In fact, it wasn't too long ago that I was in the place you may find yourself right now—a bundle of untapped potential.

In the next chapter, I'll share my journey to tapping into that potential and then unleashing my influence in the world. You have unlimited potential, and I'm excited for you to embark on this path!

Just remember—it's a *journey*, not a *destination*. This book will be your trusty guide throughout the process. Are you ready?

LET'S REVIEW

- ❖ Living life by design is about living in alignment with your Truth and your life's purpose.
- ❖ You've been blessed with gifts that *only you* can share with the world.
- ❖ It's abnormal to live out of alignment with your Truth and your purpose. Living life by default contradicts your purpose here.
- ❖ When you're in a state of living life by default, you're disconnected from your Source. This causes a lack of inspiration and fulfillment.
- ❖ The first step to living life by design is to uncover your gifts.
- ❖ The second step is being courageous and bold enough to say "Hell yeah!" to your calling.
- ❖ The final step is committing to becoming the best damn version of yourself so that you can fulfill your mission.

TAKE ACTION NOW

1. Reflect on whether you're currently living life by design or by default. If you're living life by default, what are some steps YOU CAN take to get out of the rut and back into alignment with your purpose?

2. Make the commitment to uncovering your gifts and purpose in life, if you haven't done so already. Say a prayer of intention and specifically ask God to send you the people and resources that will help you along your path. Then be on the lookout because they will begin to appear.

3. One you've discovered your purpose, say "Hell yeah!" and think of one small step you can take this week to start moving toward fulfilling it.

CHAPTER 3

MY JOURNEY TO BECOMING AN UNSTOPPABLE INFLUENCER

*The two most important days in your life are the day
you are born and the day you find out why.*

~ Mark Twain

Never in a million years would I have guessed that I'd write a book like this, or that I'd have a business serving clients around the world, much less that I would lead a movement of Influencers who would positively transform millions of lives.

That said, I knew I was a leader from a young age. Whether it was founding the Memphis chapter of the New Kids on the Block fan club in the fifth grade, starting a church youth group, or inventing a "sorority" (Delta Kappa Beta) in the seventh grade, I was frequently in leadership positions.

No matter where I was—sports, school, or my personal life—leadership positions always seemed to find me. For me, leadership was never about power or being the "boss." What really fueled me was creating a supportive environment that served others.

AN INCONVENIENT REALIZATION

After graduating from Southern Methodist University, I wasn't sure what to do with my life—or with my degrees in advertising and political science, so I went to law school.

After successfully passing the Tennessee Bar Exam, I joined a law firm. I remember one day, a couple of years into my practice, watching older partners walk by my office.

I thought, *Damn! Is that going to be me someday? I have to do this? Every. Single. Day…for the next 40 years?*

My heart chimed in and said, *Uhh uhh, girl…no freaking way! That's not you.*

But my head said, *What the Hell else are you supposed to do? You're single. No husband in sight. You just spent $100,000 of Daddy's money on law school, passed the bar, and NOW you want to quit? No way. That's not how we do things around here.*

And with that, I talked myself out of an inspired life.

I resigned myself to doing what I thought I was supposed to do, even though it was unfulfilling and didn't use my gifts in the highest and best way.

Have you ever felt that way?

Here's the thing—I knew that writing, marketing, and leadership were my gifts, but I didn't know *how* I was supposed to use them.

So while I was stuck in a job that didn't light my fire, I started seeking opportunities to use my gifts in other ways.

In the fall of 2005, after Hurricane Katrina hit the Gulf Coast, my sorority sister and I started a stuffed-animal drive called Bear Hugs with Love to support the youngest survivors. Using our gifts, our little two-city stuffed-animal drive turned into an international effort that collected and delivered over 10,000 stuffed animals to the Gulf Coast. How cool is that?

That one experience showed me the enormous impact that two women can make when they tap into their gifts and are open to inspiration. It was a game-changer. I was *hooked* and wanted to do even more, so I committed to seeking more opportunities to use my gifts.

As a result, opportunities were drawn to me like a magnet.

A LIFE-CHANGING OPPORTUNITY

The following spring, I had an opportunity to start a home business. I'd never even *considered* being an entrepreneur, but when I discovered there were people making lots of money from home, I was intrigued.

No boss? No billable hours? Fab vacations? And I would get to change people's lives?

"Sign me up!" I said.

I was *so* excited to share my discovery with everyone I knew.

I can build my own business from home, and enjoy time and financial freedom. Who wouldn't want that?

Unfortunately, my family and friends weren't exactly receptive to the message—in fact, they thought I'd lost my mind.

"Why not just stick to being a lawyer?" they said.

The reality was that I'd been bitten by the entrepreneurial bug and was done just settling in life.

So I decided to change course and share my message with complete strangers. I placed classified ads in newspapers, purchased billboard space on a highway, and even cold-called home-business leads. None of those methods worked for me.

By all accounts, my entrepreneurial endeavor was a complete flop. Yet the flame had been lit, and there was *nothing* that would stop me from building a business. Or so I thought...

One day, Rich and I were doing some internet research and discovered the world of online marketing, and more importantly, how to attract the perfect prospects to our business and never face rejection again.

Within three months of marketing our business online, we began making sales. We started building a team, and checks began arriving in the mail. We were stoked! We were making "mailbox money" just for helping other people!

At the time, Rich was still working as an advertising executive for Fortune 500 brands, and I was still practicing law full-time. But as more checks started to arrive, we doubled down on our business-building efforts.

We'd come home around 6 or 7 p.m., work on our business until 1 or 2 a.m., then start the whole cycle over again the following day. This routine continued for 18 months. Soon we were consistently making $2,000 to $3,000 per month, and our income was growing. I figured that I would finally be able to quit my job within a year.

THE SUCKER PUNCH

Then I got an email from the primary company we were promoting at the time. Turns out they no longer wanted their distributors to use the internet for marketing. That was a *huge* gut punch. But then they took it a step further.

The company gave me a whopping 48 hours to delete *all* the content I'd created over the past 18 months, or our position with the company would be terminated.

I. Was. Devastated.

I wish I could tell you that I mustered up the Tony Robbins within, took the bump in stride, and kept going—but I can't.

I quit our business.

I gave up.

I figured that I'd just practice law and ditch my dream of being a full-time entrepreneur. Fortunately, Rich had an insatiable hunger to build a successful business, so he continued working on it while I licked my wounds on the sidelines.

Eighteen months later, I was done pouting and decided to rejoin Rich in the business. This time I was on a mission. I'd lost my last business because I had been promoting another company's brand instead of my own.

I had learned my lesson and wanted to share it with others. I didn't want anyone else's hard work to be ruined like mine had been, so I began teaching home-business owners how to build their own personal brand—one that belonged to *them*, and not to some company.

Rich and I launched our first digital training program in the fall of 2010, and when we attracted our first customer, we literally jumped for joy.

"Someone thought we were valuable! We put our knowledge into print, and someone bought it!" I shouted while running around the house acting as if Ed McMahon had showed up with a big check from Publisher's Clearing House.

Life got even more exciting when we started making sales of our product in our sleep. Those were SWISS dollars, as author Dan Miller calls them—Sales While I Sleep Soundly.[3]

From that moment on, there was no turning back.

Within six months, I was honored as a Top Blogger in the home-business industry. We had a group of private coaching clients and were making sales online like clockwork.

Soon after, we began winning Top Producer awards, were invited to speaking gigs around the country, and more and more people began coming to us for help.

The best was yet to come, though.

THE CALLING

One December morning, while reading my morning devotional, I felt "called" to quit my job. Upon getting this rather unusual calling, I did what any rational, left-brained attorney would do in this situation.

I freaked out!

My head told me that I was just making up the calling. Why in the *world* would I quit my cushy, full-time law gig to take on the risk of being an entrepreneur full-time?

Rich had taken on the risk by quitting *his* job, but I mitigated that by having a full-time income.

But no. That's not how my life was supposed to be, even though it seemed perfectly reasonable in my own mind.

The reality was that I had a special purpose that required my full-time attention. I had to be "all in" to make the impact I was intending to make. (If this part intrigues you, I'll be sharing more of this story in Chapter 10.)

So ultimately, I said "Hell yeah!" to the mission, and put all my faith in God to show us the way to grow our business. I also committed to growing into a person who is *capable* of being a full-time entrepreneur.

I sought out business mentors and doubled up on my spiritual and personal development training.

Sure enough, God provided the path and the resources I needed, and the following year, at the age of 33, I quit my full-time job as an attorney. A few months later, we released my signature program, *Branded: 100% Authentic*, a digital home-study program that helps entrepreneurs define, build, and monetize their authentic brands online.

One year later, Rich and I hosted our first live event, where we welcomed attendees from across the United States and Canada. At the event, I sold our first year-long mentorship program, and we had so many people jump at the chance to work with us, we made $50,000 in a single day.

It was mind-blowing money. That month, we generated over $70,000 from our business—more than my entire annual salary as an associate attorney! At that moment, I realized the power and magnitude of what we had created.

You'd think that this was the beginning of our Unstoppable rise to the top of the success ladder, and that the hard work was done because we had it all figured out.

But that's not how this cookie crumbles.

Of course, on Facebook, my friends and followers saw pictures of fabulous trips, speaking engagements, and tons of clients, but I was fighting my own secret battle filled with self-sabotaging behaviors and limiting beliefs.

* * * * * *

A lifetime of disordered eating (binge, diet, binge, diet) had turned into just binge, binge, and more binge. If I had to pinpoint one trigger on top of a general lack of self-esteem, it had to be my inability to get pregnant.

My desire to be a mom started at a very young age. I treated my brother, who was seven years my junior, like my own child. When I finally found Mr. Right, at the age of 26, I looked forward to quickly starting a family.

I started trying to get pregnant immediately after we got married. After nearly a year of unsuccessful attempts, my doctor prescribed the fertility drug Clomid, and again we tried. Month after month our pregnancy attempts failed.

Our move to Boise took my mind off of my failure to become a mother, but only temporarily. As soon as we were settled in our new home, we visited one of the world's top fertility specialists, Dr. Russell Foulk, and he delivered the bad news: I had Stage 4 endometriosis and a hydrosalpinx, which meant the "fingers" of my fallopian tube were scarred together and wouldn't carry an egg. In fact, it was one of the worst cases he'd seen, and I needed immediate surgery so they could cut one of my tubes.

The news got worse. My other fallopian tube was scarred shut as well, so according to him I would never become a mother naturally. As Dr. Foulk spoke, my heart sank.

I was ashamed. I felt like a failure as a woman and a wife. I believed that women were designed to carry a child and wives then become mothers, so I was failing on all fronts. Fortunately, due to advances in technology, Dr. Foulk told us that we were perfect candidates for in vitro fertilization (IVF).

After my surgery, I was cleared to start fertility treatments. For the first time in years, I felt hopeful that I would become a mother.

I started taking rounds of fertility shots. Then came the egg removal, and ultimately the embryo transfer. Anyone who's been through fertility treatments will tell you, the waiting is *excruciating*. Throughout the wait, I kept myself busy by reading baby books and shopping for nursery furniture.

A few days later, I took a pregnancy test, and our dreams had come true—we were pregnant!

I started planning our big baby reveal. A few days later, I knew something was wrong. It was. Instead of spending time at Babies 'R Us, I ended up in the ER— no longer pregnant.

To add insult to injury, my precious grandmother, Teta, died a couple of weeks later. Her death was followed by the murder of my childhood priest, Father Ed, who years before had flown into town to marry me and Rich. That was the final straw.

I drowned my sadness in food. What had been a weight gain of only 10 pounds after our wedding turned into 30, and it didn't stop there. People allowed me to use my infertility treatments and stress levels as excuses to gain weight, drink wine, and eat extremely large amounts of chocolate.

A second IVF attempt also ended in a trip to the emergency room and no child.

Looking back, I never allowed myself the opportunity to grieve our miscarriage or my infertility. As more and more of my friends got pregnant and had babies, my shame and lack of confidence grew.

Do you know what else grew? My waist size.

THE BIG, FAT, UGLY TRUTH

Before I knew it, I had tipped the scales at 210 pounds. I was officially obese. I hated shopping because my go-to stores didn't carry clothes in sizes 16 or 18. I no longer enjoyed going out with friends because I was always tired, plus I cringed at the frumpy clothes I had to wear. I dreaded being in pictures because, in my mind, I was the token fat girl in every shot.

That hatred started affecting our business too. As the chief content creator, I wasn't doing anything to help our business grow. I fulfilled the deliverables to our existing clients, but I didn't want to do anything else, so our growth flat-lined. We still made an enviable income, but it wasn't at the level it should have been.

Finally, after nearly seven years of waiting, we were blessed with the birth of our precious daughter. Her arrival gave me the perfect excuse to essentially ignore our business. A year later, although I was filled with the joy of motherhood, the feelings of shame, lack of self-confidence, and unworthiness bubbled back to the surface.

Once again, I felt like a failure—as a wife, as a mother, and as a coach and mentor—because I was hiding a secret: I lacked self-confidence and I felt worthless. So worthless that I was barely in *any* of the pictures that we took of our daughter. I was too ashamed. I didn't want to ruin the photos, because she was so beautiful, and I wasn't.

My struggles and repeated failures to become a mother had shattered my self-confidence and caused me to doubt my ability to help others. After all, I couldn't even help myself.

HITTING ROCK BOTTOM

Things went from bad to worse.

I was uninspired. I'd lost my drive and my passion to serve others. Rich and I fought frequently about our business because of my lack of involvement.

One afternoon in particular, I leaned against our kitchen counter and sobbed to Rich. "I just want to walk away from *everything*. I don't *want* to coach our clients. I don't *want* to teach another web class. I don't *want* to inspire anyone. I just *want* to go back to my job—that's it."

"But what about your calling?" Rich asked, knowing this was the one thing that *usually* snapped me out of a funk like this.

"God picked the wrong damn girl for the job!" I whimpered through the tears.

The week following my meltdown wasn't much better. I was like a zombie. I felt empty because I had nothing left to give. I had nothing to give my husband, my clients, or my friends or family.

Everything I had left in me, I gave to our daughter—the precious soul I had waited for patiently for seven long years.

What's wrong with you? shouted the voice in my head. *You have what you want—what else is there? Don't be selfish. Just get yourself together!*

But I couldn't.

I just couldn't do it anymore.

Another week went by, and I was faced with an important decision. I had already purchased tickets to attend a business conference in San Diego, and it was time to go. Would I forfeit the conference fees and the money for a plane ticket and hotel room, or would I just suck it up and go?

In my heart, I knew that if I wanted to have a *chance* of getting out of my funk, I needed to attend this event. After all, Marcus Lemonis—my all-time favorite TV business mentor—would be there.

So on a wing and a prayer, I packed my bags and headed to San Diego for the three-day conference.

The first two days sparked a little fire within me, but it was quickly snuffed out by day's end.

THE EPIPHANY

On the morning of the third day, I only had a tiny shred of hope that the inspiration I sought would appear. It looked like I was headed back to my job and admitting defeat as an entrepreneur again.

Then out walked Marcus Lemonis. He asked the audience one simple question:

> "What's one thing that you've never told anybody, and how does it relate to your business?"

In that moment, surrounded by 1,500 strangers, the answer washed over me.

I hate myself.

There. I said it.

The truth was that when I looked at myself in the mirror, I *literally* hated the person staring back at me. Despised her.

I thought, *Now how did that little gem affect our business?*

The answer was as plain as day.

It was the sole reason our business hadn't grown over the past three years. I didn't feel worthy enough to inspire or lead others. I felt like a *complete* fraud.

After all, I hated myself. And if anyone knew that, they wouldn't want to learn from me, much less do business with us. So I had refused to create content for our followers. I had refused to support Rich in our business.

The sad reality was that I was the flat tire on our bicycle, and I was making poor Rich pedal for the both of us, all the while bitching about how slow we were going.

That epiphany was just the beginning. The Truth continued to wash over me as Marcus spoke about the importance of reinvention. The little voice allowed me to see my own reality in a way I'd never seen it before.

The 55 pounds of fat I'd piled on over the years? That was a physical manifestation of the hatred I had for myself, for the fact that I was infertile and that I wasn't as slim or as pretty as my competitors.

In that moment, as Marcus continued talking in the background, I was filled with light and my Truth. God blessed me that day with clarity, and I seized that moment and made one simple decision.

I wanted the fat and the corresponding hatred gone. Now.

I wanted to LOVE myself. I wanted to be the REAL and authentic Natasha. Not the person who cowers behind bars of chocolate, glasses of wine, and pints of ice cream. I wanted to step out and shine.

For the first time in years, I felt alive. I felt light. I felt infinite joy. I knew where I was headed—a complete and total reinvention—and I knew the first step I needed to take.

As I sat on the plane waiting to take off for Boise, I pulled out my iPhone, opened Facebook, and typed this message to the hard-core nutrition coach that I'd been thinking of contacting (and had been Facebook stalking) for months.

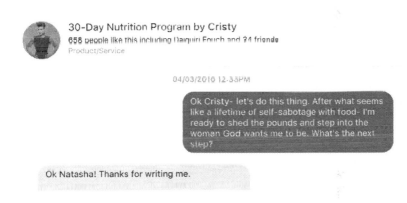

30-Day Nutrition Program by Cristy
658 people like this including Daiquiri Fouch and 24 friends
Product/Service

04/03/2016 12:33PM

Ok Cristy- let's do this thing. After what seems like a lifetime of self-sabotage with food- I'm ready to shed the pounds and step into the woman God wants me to be. What's the next step?

Ok Natasha! Thanks for writing me.

I knew I had made the right decision. I wanted the fat gone, and Cristy was the right woman for the job. That didn't make the next 18 hours any easier, though. *How hard would this be?* I wondered. *How long will it take? Can I really do this?*

My emotions flip-flopped, from excitement one minute to sheer panic the next. But ultimately, I decided that a radical change was necessary if I wanted to be the woman God intended me to be.

THE REINVENTION BEGINS

At 8:30 a.m. the following day, I walked into Cristy "Code Red" Nickel's office and broke down in tears as I shared my journey to becoming clinically obese. Then I handed her a check and mentally congratulated myself on taking the all-important first step of my reinvention.

Over the next five and a half months, I shed *every single one* of those 55 pounds of hatred. When I looked in the mirror, I finally saw who I really was—a woman whose light was shining bright.

All it took was one decision, that's it. The decision to get back to my core Truth, so I could reignite my candle and allow it to shine brightly again.

My journey reminds me of a quote by Jen Sincero in the best-selling book *You Are a Badass*: "[I]t's not your fault that you're f***ed up. It's your fault if you *stay* f***ed up…"[4]

* * * * * *

THE "SHIFT"

I chose to shed the ugliness of my past. I chose reinvention, and because of that brave decision, life got a whole lot sweeter.

Clients started coming to us in droves. And not just any clients—PERFECT clients.

I was a happier and more joyful wife, mother, coach, and friend. I began to walk with a pep in my step and a confidence that I never knew existed within me. I was living on purpose and with purpose.

Some think that reinvention is a bad thing. It isn't. It's a bad*ass* thing.

Guess who's in the driver's seat of your life? YOU.

Not your mom, not your dad, not your significant other. Not your kids. Not the ghosts of your past.

Not the same BS stories you've probably told yourself about why you can't live the life of your dreams.

You can have *everything* you want in life. Truly. I'd heard this concept repeatedly over the years, but I never fully believed it. Then I discovered the missing piece to the "get everything you want" puzzle.

A decision.

You can get everything you want in life and you can make the impact you're intended to make—ONE decision is all it takes to get started!

In fact, you will have one very important decision to make before the end of this chapter. But first, there are a few questions you must consider.

- ❖ Are you willing to say YES to the gifts that God has given you?
- ❖ Are you ready to sift through the B.S. life has handed to you to find the lessons?
- ❖ Are you ready to reignite your flame, and keep it burning bright every single day for the rest of your life?

❖ Are you ready to share that light with the world?

If your answers are YES, you're ready to make the ONE decision that will transform your life. It's the decision to live life as an Unstoppable Influencer. So if you're ready to make that decision, I want you to say out loud right now…

I AM AN UNSTOPPABLE INFLUENCER.

I'm not joking. Say it!

I AM AN UNSTOPPABLE INFLUENCER.

Yes, I'm talking to you! You may be in bed with your significant other asleep next to you. You may be reading this on an airplane, in a coffee shop, or by the pool.

Say the words.

I AM AN UNSTOPPABLE INFLUENCER.

Now say it like you *mean* it.

I AM AN UNSTOPPABLE INFLUENCER.

One more time.

I AM AN UNSTOPPABLE INFLUENCER.

Yes, friend. Yes you are.

Welcome to an elite group. Here is our Manifesto.

We're Unstoppable Influencers...

- ❖ We share our God-given gifts with the world. We're experts in our fields. We're on a mission to positively influence people's lives. So come along for the ride, or get out of our way!
- ❖ We're committed to expanding our sphere of influence so we can make a big impact. We inspire and uplift others daily.
- ❖ We're perfectly imperfect. We tackle fear and self-doubt like a BOSS.
- ❖ We don't let our light dim, even in the winds of adversity. We wear the armor of our Truth and equip ourselves with tools and lessons that allow our light to shine bright, *no matter what*.
- ❖ We are not victims. We're eternal students looking for the lessons gifted to us in challenges.
- ❖ We're action takers. We do the work we're intended to do and make NO EXCUSES.
- ❖ We know that to unleash our influence in the world, we must step outside our comfort zone. We HAVE FAITH, and we'll DO things even when we're scared.
- ❖ We use our INFLUENCE FOR GOOD. We know our worth and charge accordingly.
- ❖ We know that by sharing our gifts with the world, we'll have everything we want in life. If you want to join our movement, ONE DECISION is all it takes—the decision to LIVE LIFE as an Unstoppable Influencer.

I AM AN UNSTOPPABLE INFLUENCER.

Yes you are!

Now that you've made your decision, the next step to getting everything you want in life and fulfilling your calling is being willing to shift your mindset. I'll show you how in the following chapters. Then just act on the strategies I teach you and you'll be set!

TAKE ACTION NOW

1. Write out your story, and look for themes and patterns. Let your instinct guide how far back your story should go. For the purpose of this exercise, just allow yourself to begin writing (or typing) without editing.

2. What lessons have you learned that can help others on their paths?

3. Commit to your role as an Unstoppable Influencer. Print out the Unstoppable Influencer Manifesto at UnstoppableInfluence.com/manifesto and display it in your office as a reminder of your greatness. You can also download the image and save it to your desktop or smartphone!

CHAPTER 4

HOW TO BECOME UNSTOPPABLE

The question isn't who is going to let me;
it's who is going to stop me

~ Ayn Rand

Now is your time to shine. Not tomorrow. Not when the kids are grown. Not when you retire.

It's no accident that you picked up this book, because you were intended to read it. If this sounds a bit far-fetched, stick with me and I'll explain.

It wasn't that long ago that I was where you may find your-self right now—you know you're awesome at *something,* but you're not getting paid what you're worth.

Perhaps you know you've got a message to share with the world, yet you can't help but look at others in your industry that may be…

- ❖ More established
- ❖ More attractive
- ❖ More comfortable on video

Or they may have...

+ A better website
+ A fancier office
+ More impressive credentials
+ More money
+ More clients

This causes you to think, "Why should I even bother? I'll never be as good/successful/impactful as so-and-so."

To make yourself feel better, you continue purchasing training programs and attending conferences, without ever *really* taking action to put yourself out there in a meaningful way.

Or perhaps you *are* an action taker, but you've hit the proverbial wall. You're slammed with business, but are burning the midnight oil and not getting paid like you should.

Maybe your level of influence and impact appears to have hit a ceiling because you can't work harder. You're frustrated because you know you're meant to be bigger than you are, but you don't know how to get there. I want you to know that you're not the only one. Let me introduce you to one of my clients.

MEET CRISTY

When I met Cristy for the first time, I was enchanted by her passion for her clients and the long list of success stories from her nutrition program.

I knew that hiring Cristy to help me lose the 55 pounds I'd packed on would be the last time I would ever go on a program to lose that much weight. That's because when Cristy worked with clients, they got massive results: they lost a ton of weight *and* took their lives back. I wanted that. I *needed* that.

So I hired Cristy and she held my hand every single day for the next 30 days. The result? I lost 20 pounds of fat, and my body fat percentage decreased by 8%. I was no longer obese!

I should have been ecstatic, but instead I felt guilty. I'd only paid Cristy a measly $500, although the value I had received was off the charts. As a business coach, I felt an obligation to tell her she was undercharging, so I did.

As I went in for my 30-day measurements, I asked Cristy if it was okay to give her a few suggestions for her business. Her face lit up.

"Of *course*! I know all about you. I'm ready to take notes—teach me."

I was a little taken aback by this response, until I discovered that she had *googled* me. Apparently, Cristy had been unsatisfied with my generic comment that I "owned a business." So she went online and found my website. She watched my training videos, and apparently was hoping I would give her some business and marketing advice.

In my heart, I knew that Cristy was meant to be much bigger than just a local nutritionist. In fact, her backstory was the reason I was excited to work with her.

Cristy was a former professional boxer. *The Ring* magazine had named her one of the "Top 3 Most Dangerous Females on the Planet." I decided I needed someone that hard-core to keep me accountable and keep the chocolate and wine out of my hands.

She had been featured on MTV's show *MADE*, and was a celebrity personal trainer who worked with stars like Katie Couric, Ethan Hawke, and Claire Danes. In fact, *Allure* magazine did an entire story on her after naming her New York's Best Personal Trainer.

Cristy's story is fascinating. After declining the opportunity to work on NBC's *The Biggest Loser*, she moved from New York to her home state of Idaho to work with clients not as a personal trainer, but as a nutritionist. She quickly became *the* go-to person in Idaho for people who wanted to lose weight for good and transform their lives.

For all the outward success and accolades Cristy had accumulated over the years, she was working around the clock for her clients, spending less and less time with her husband, and only making around $30,000 a year.

So when I looked at Cristy that day in her office and said, "There's absolutely *no* reason for you to be making *any* less than $100,000 per year," her mouth dropped open. She said, "You have *got* to be kidding me!"

I wasn't.

In Cristy's mind, she couldn't work any harder than she already was, so if she wasn't putting in more hours, how could she *possibly* make more money?

I had the answer.

The reality was that Cristy was re-igniting people's light with her influence an average of 12 times per month—144 lives per year. She was making an impact, for sure. But I knew she had the potential to impact *millions*.

I asked Cristy if she was willing to become the person God intended *her* to be. She said yes, and with that, Cristy joined my year-long *Premier* coaching program.

She decided to spread her light further than just Idaho, and at a faster rate. Cristy didn't know how to do it on her own, so she finally sought the help she needed.

Within 30 days of working with me, Cristy had tripled her income and was working less than she had been before. By the end of the year, Cristy hit the coveted six-figure mark.

Within 12 months, Cristy's former *annual* income had become her *monthly* income, and she was impacting *thousands* of lives in the process—while working a *fraction* of the time.

Finally, she was able to enjoy more time with her husband, Miles, and dog, Annabelle, who had both been pushed to the side for the past couple of years.

That's incredible, right? Guess what? This is possible for you, too!

Cristy's journey started with one decision—to become an Unstoppable Influencer.

She embraced her giftedness, acknowledged that her sphere of influence was intended to be exponentially greater, and committed herself to doing the work necessary NOW to fulfill her mission as an Unstoppable Influencer.

BURNING THE BRIDGE

Your first step to becoming Unstoppable is committing to the role of an Unstoppable Influencer. And then you "burn the bridge."

Burning the Bridge is a concept I've taught for years. It's allegedly based on a military tactic where, if a leader knew their troops were scared to go into battle, they would order them to burn the bridge they had just crossed. When retreat was no longer an option, the troops fought harder and won.

You've accepted the honor and duty of sharing your light with the world on a larger scale, so to be Unstoppable, you'll have to burn the bridge.

You may be wondering, "How large of a scale are we talking about, Natasha?"

Well, the scope of influence varies from person to person. You may be intended to influence your town, state, or country, or maybe the world.

The world needs Influencers of all shapes and sizes, men and women, young and old. It takes Influencers of various races, religions, and sexual orientations. Unstoppable Influence knows no borders or single language.

As I've said, we're all here *on* purpose and *for* a purpose. Like many, you may have started out playing small, because it's safe.

You didn't want to put yourself out there too much, because what if you fail?

But you will no longer allow small-time thinking to hold you back. The time is **NOW**. *Your* time is now!

It's time to play a bigger game and step outside your comfort zone to make your intended impact. Like Cristy, you'll need to "burn the bridge" and commit to becoming the Influencer you are capable of being.

So what else *do* you need to do to become an Unstoppable Influencer?

Keep reading, and I'll show you.

Just know that I'm here for you and you're in awesome company. It is my intention that thousands will read this book and join our movement of Unstoppable Influencers—all shining their light in the world.

Every journey begins with a first step, and yours starts right now.

LET'S REVIEW

+ Unstoppable Influencers know that NOW is the time to shine. Not later.
+ Unstoppable Influence knows no borders.
+ You become an Unstoppable Influencer the day you decide that you're committed to stepping into that role and then "burn the bridge."

* You must step outside your comfort zone to make your intended impact.

* The scope of your influence may vary. The size does not matter. What matters is that you deliver your message.

TAKE ACTION NOW

1. Pray or meditate on the intended scope of your influence.

2. If you haven't done so already, download your copy of the *Unstoppable Influence Companion Workbook* for FREE at UnstoppableInfluence.com/gift then read and sign the Unstoppable Influencer Pledge in the workbook and declare, "I'm burning the bridge!"

3. Go to UnstoppableInfluence.com/group and join our Unstoppable Influencer community. Introduce yourself, and declare your commitment to sharing your gift with the world.

CHAPTER 5

UNBECOMING

Maybe the journey isn't so much about becoming anything. Maybe it's about un-becoming everything that isn't really you, so you can be who you were meant to be in the first place.

~ Unknown

I think you're born with it—Influencer DNA.

The tricky part is that just because you were born with it doesn't mean you *know* you were born with it.

Case in point: Did 14-month-old Michael Jordan *know* he'd be the best basketball player of all time? Did 5-year-old Steve Jobs know he'd create the Apple empire?

Hell no.

As you start engaging in the game of life, the Universe throws you hints along the way about your purpose. If you haven't uncovered your purpose yet, no worries—we'll cover this in Chapter 10.

Just know that once you accept your role as an Influencer, there's another step you must take. It's a little thing I like to call "letting shit go."

LET IT GO

If you don't let stuff go, your light can't shine brightly because it's being covered up. Without an unobstructed light, you can't pass your flame to others. And if you're not passing the flame, you aren't influencing the world.

So what needs to go, and how does that impact your ability to become an Unstoppable Influencer?

Great question! Glad you asked.

Think of it this way: From the time you're old enough to understand what people are saying, their comments or actions can impact you deeply, to the core of your subconscious mind. Here's the kicker—this can happen *without* you consciously being aware of it.

How messed up is that?!?

For example, after one of my Emotion Code[5] sessions (a cool thing to try, by the way), I discovered that my feelings of never being "good enough" originated in the second grade. The second. Effing. Grade.

I had taken on this emotion after my achievement test results indicated that I was merely *average* compared to most of my friends.

At that moment, poor seven-year-old Natasha felt for the first time that she wasn't good enough. That dark emotion dimmed my light slightly, and I didn't realize it for 31 freakin' years!

Then there was the little punk in the fifth grade who called me "Hairy Legs." It wasn't my fault that I had darker, more noticeable hair than my blonde friends (damn Lebanese genes). With that, I was introduced to a little emotion called *insecurity*.

Then there was the time my mother recounted a story about when I was two, and she overheard two women saying, "What a shame that she has a crossed eye, otherwise she is such a pretty baby," and how it broke her heart to hear someone make such mean comments about me.

Why hello, shame and disappointment, come on in and join the party!

These are just three tiny examples of moments in my life where I was consciously *unaware* of the dimming impact they had on my light.

Of course, there were other events that consciously screwed me up too—being body shamed by loved ones, the death of family members, years of infertility, a miscarriage—so it's no wonder that I had packed on so much weight that I tipped the scales at 210 pounds.

It was a really rough time. I had severe acid reflux, couldn't sleep, and was always sick. I had lost all inspiration and motivation to build our business. I'd pretty much turned into a hermit, which was totally abnormal for an extrovert like me.

I was ashamed to attend social events, because the only outfits that fit me were size 16 or 18, which was a stark contrast to my former 8/10.

Plus, I hated being the token fat girl in everyone's pictures. So instead, I stayed home and cooked awesome meals for my husband. We drank fine wine, and enjoyed pretty much any and every dessert we craved. My eating habits spiraled out of control as I continued to medicate myself with food.

The bigger I got, the more shame, insecurity, and unworthiness strangled me.

When I finally became a mom after seven long years of waiting, every ounce of light within me went to caring for my baby girl, because I wanted to give her *everything*.

Then one day, I made a painful realization. Looking back on the first 10 months of our daughter's life, I noticed there were barely any pictures of me. My shame had kept me behind the camera because of my fear of ruining the pictures.

You know from my story in Chapter 3 that a few weeks later, I awakened to my Truth—the fat on my body was a physical manifestation of the hatred I had for myself, and I wanted it gone. Pronto.

That bold decision was the big domino that fell, triggering an amazing and perfect chain reaction of events I can only describe as my journey of *unbecoming*.

Fat, depressed Natasha wasn't the real, authentic me. Scared, insecure, unworthy Natasha wasn't me either. That was who I'd *become* over the years, so I needed to engage in some serious unbecoming, *fast*.

There was pretty much nothing I wouldn't try to "unbecome" the sad, dark person I was. Energy clearing, body coding, fasting, hypnosis (more on this in Chapter 7), coaching, books, crystals... You name it, I tried it. I was ready to shed the darkness and step into the light.

You have to try whatever works for you, because you'll "unbecome" in your own way and in your own time. In fact, there's a damn good chance that the *you* reading this right now isn't the "real" you.

I mean, sure, you're *you*. If you get pulled over for speeding today, the cop will tell you that you're *you*. But for a moment, just entertain the thought that perhaps you're not the *real* YOU, the one who's in alignment with your Truth.

Since you're still reading, and haven't thrown this book across the room because of the last few paragraphs, let me tell you something. There are Truths within you that are ready to come out and shine bright.

Another thing you need to know is this—if you've been through a colossal shitstorm up until now, you're not alone.

In fact, most Unstoppable Influencers have had really awful experiences—rape, molestation, kidnapping, brain tumors, homelessness, or physical or emotional abuse. Those are just *some* of the experiences that my powerful Influencer friends have had.

I suppose it's like some kind of screwed-up rite of passage. It can dim your light for a while, and then as soon as you "awaken" and begin the process of unbecoming, your Truth will be revealed.

So what does that mean for *you* right now?

To align with your Truth, you're going to have to stare some ugly memories in the face, and then release them.

You're going to have to acknowledge that you can't do the work of unbecoming alone. If you could, you would've already done it. *Everyone* needs help in the unbecoming process. It's not a sign of weakness; it's a sign of strength.

Once you're really, truly, balls-to-the-wall committed to letting go everything that's no longer in alignment with your Truth, miracles are going to happen, friend.

Just watch as the resources and support you need show up in your life. Just like magic.

Be prepared, though.

FILLING THE VOID

The unbecoming process will not only force you to let go (including people, jobs, food, alcohol, and drugs), it'll fill the void left behind with glorious gifts, such as friends you never would have met and opportunities that were just waiting for the real *you* to show up.

In fact, if you've been single, watch out—your soulmate will likely be right around the corner. Miracles are going to happen, I tell ya!

When you've stripped away all the BS, and you're left with just your naked, beautiful Truth, this is where your light is going to shine so freaking bright. People will notice and be magnetically attracted to you.

People ask me all the time now, "Oooh, Natasha, you look so *fabulous*! What's your secret?"

I'm walking in my Truth. That's my secret.

Sometimes, if they're ready to awaken and for their candle to be lit, they'll ask for guidance. I'm *always* happy to share my flame, because in moments like this, I can see my influence starting a gorgeous cascading effect of pure light in the world. You can do the same!

LET'S REVIEW

* Not everyone was born with Influencer DNA.
* In order to become who you truly are, you'll have to "unbecome" everything you're not.
* Everyone needs help in the unbecoming process. You don't have to fly solo.
* When you let stuff go, you'll make room for miracles, beauty, and abundance in your life.
* When you're stripped down to your naked, beautiful Truth, your light will shine the brightest.

TAKE ACTION NOW

1. As you read this chapter, some memories of your life were likely triggered. Write these down in the *Unstoppable Influence Companion Workbook*, then reflect on how these memories had a positive or negative impact on your light.

2. Make a list of everything you think needs to be released to start your process of unbecoming. If you think you don't have baggage, quit lying to yourself. Everyone has baggage. Spend some time meditating, and ask your Source to reveal areas where you may be blocked.

3. If you've never had an energy clearing or Emotion Code session, consider getting one. If this sounds completely wacky to you, it's all the more reason for you to try it. The worst-case scenario is that you don't feel any different. But in the best-case scenario, you will get some icky subconscious blocks released *without* having to go through years of therapy. Yay!

   I've listed a few resources (and additional information about energy clearings and the Emotion Code) in the *Companion Workbook*. If you haven't done so already, you can download your copy of the *Unstoppable Influence Companion Workbook* for FREE at UnstoppableInfluence.com/gift

CHAPTER 6

YOUR NEW LIFE AS AN UNSTOPPABLE INFLUENCER

There is no passion to be found playing small—in settling for a life that is less than the one you are capable of living.

~ Nelson Mandela

There's no way to sugarcoat it—the life of an Unstoppable Influencer is just different. Be prepared for that. We're a different breed. When I said it's an elite group, I meant it.

Elite means that the vast majority of your family, friends, and coworkers won't become a part of this group. They won't understand it.

Some will support your journey, but most will not. It's sad but true.

As an Unstoppable Influencer, you're operating at a different frequency than the rest of the world. You're tapping into a gift and light that others don't necessarily know or understand. That's okay. It doesn't mean that you're better and they're worse, or that you're good and they're bad. It's just *different*.

You've likely already experienced this to some degree, especially if you've already started your own business.

THE INEVITABLE BEGINS...

People may start judging you. One of my friends told me I was "obsessed with money" because I was working so many hours in our business while practicing law full-time.

Others felt I was selfish for not being satisfied with such a "prestigious" profession.

Then there were people who tried to make us feel guilty for spending so much time working. Of course, there were others who expressed the concern by asking repeatedly, "Are you making money yet?" in a passive-aggressive attempt to express their displeasure, knowing that we were.

Other people may cast all their fears and anxieties on you by sharing their "concerns" about your choice to pursue this path.

- ❖ "How will you balance your job, family obligations, AND this new project?"
- ❖ "You do know that one in five businesses fail within the first five years, right?"
- ❖ "How do you have the time and money to start ANOTHER new venture?"
- ❖ This last one is my personal pet peeve—the classic shaming method: "Oh, you're starting ANOTHER business? What is it this time?"

Here's the thing you need to realize about people's opinions: most of them mean well. They're not making comments to intentionally hurt you. They're operating based upon the stories in their *own* heads or from their own Egos (more on this in Chapter 7).

People look at life through their own lenses. Those lenses are clouded by their personal fears, anxieties, and shortcomings, so they are transferring their own feelings to you.

What they say may be 100% true for them, but that doesn't make it true for you.

Something else to consider is that people are inherently concerned with themselves first and you second.

Your success is a mirror—it highlights your accomplishments but can reflect their failures. They may be afraid that their relationship with you will change when you get "bigger" or more "successful."

Another thing to prepare for is that while you're in a massive growth phase, reading tons of personal development books, listening to podcasts, and going to seminars, your friends' conversations about the latest Kanye antics or the contestants on this season of *The Voice* may start to irritate you.

You want to share the life-changing information you're learning, but your friends just want to bitch about their spouses, kids, and jobs. Or they want to discuss topics that seem so trivial now that you're focused on unleashing your influence in the world.

Going out drinking three nights a week no longer seems appealing, because you'd rather get home to watch an online webinar or read the hot new book you just ordered from Amazon.

One thing is for certain: Life will change for you, and that's good. Remember that there's a season for everything—including relationships.

If you're no longer enjoying girls' night out, you may find yourself making more excuses to stay home. You may start getting pushback from your friends for "abandoning" the crew. That's okay, you don't need to apologize for your choices.

Just know that the individuals you choose to surround yourself with regularly will determine your scope of influence. If you surround yourself with small-minded people who are playing small, your influence will be small.

If you instead choose to surround yourself with big thinkers and Unstoppable Influencers who are committed to playing a bigger game, your influence will be big.

Rich and I have invested well over a hundred thousand dollars into our business and personal development education, and most importantly in mastermind groups with big thinkers. We've made the conscious choice to surround ourselves with Unstoppable Influencers playing a big game. By surrounding ourselves with seven-, eight-, and nine-figure entrepreneurs, we're operating at a much higher level than we would have been had we spent all our time chatting about the Kardashians.

Don't read this to mean that you and I are "better" than people who choose to sit on the couch watching reality television. There's no right or wrong when it comes to living your life. All it means is that Unstoppable Influencers have different priorities.

For example, I've been called to a life of service by empowering Unstoppable Influencers to get the clarity, confidence, and strategies they need to boost their income and level of influence in the world without working longer hours.

My priorities are God first, then family, and then my tribe of Unstoppable Influencers. While I'll sneak in episodes of *The Bachelor* or *America's Got Talent* now and again, those mind-numbing activities just aren't high on my priority list anymore.

At the end of the day, it all boils down to this:

Are you committed to making the greatest impact possible during your lifetime?

If so, you'll have to make some choices. Choices about what you read, what you listen to, who you spend time with, and where you spend your money.

Be prepared that not everyone will be happy with your choices and, as a result, you may have to shed some old, unhealthy relationships in order to make room for new ones. That said, this is an exciting and exhilarating part of the journey of becoming an Unstoppable Influencer!

LET'S REVIEW

❖ Unstoppable Influencers are a different breed. We're part of an elite club.

❖ Some family members and friends will support your journey, but many will not.

❖ Your success is a mirror. It highlights your accomplishments and can reflect other people's failures.

❖ Other people's Truth may not be true for you.

❖ Who you choose to surround yourself with is a major determining factor in how big your scope of influence will be.

❖ You may have to shed some old, unhealthy habits in order to make room for new ones that are congruent with your life as an Unstoppable Influencer.

❖ As an Unstoppable Influencer, you'll have to make choices about what you read, what you listen to, who you spend time with, and where you spend your money. Your family or friends may not approve of these choices. Make them anyway.

TAKE ACTION NOW

1. Always assume positive intent when speaking with others. Don't jump to the worst-case scenario before getting all the facts.

2. Reflect on how you are currently spending your time. Do your daily tasks align with your desire to become an Unstoppable Influencer and play a bigger game?

3. Look at your circle of influence. Are the people in your life helping you move toward fulfilling your purpose, or pulling you away from it? Look on your nightstand, in iTunes, or on your Kindle. Are the books you're reading and the music you're listening to in alignment with your calling? Reflect on whether you're happy with the way your life is now. What changes do you need to make? Write down the actions you'll take and then do them. Make the changes necessary to live in alignment with your purpose.

CHAPTER 7

CLEARING THE HURDLES
TO YOUR INFLUENCE

In the middle of a difficulty lies opportunity.

~ Albert Einstein

Most Hollywood movies follow a similar storyline. A hero goes on a journey to find true love or save the world. The hero faces challenges and then ultimately achieves their goal.

Did you know there's actually a science behind that storyline?

Screenwriter Michael Hague taught the concept of the Hero's Two Journeys at a seminar I attended. It's the formula many fiction books and movies follow. In short, a hero embarks on two journeys: an outer journey and an inner journey.

The outer journey is the hero taking action to reach their ultimate goal. The inner journey is one of personal transformation that results in the hero becoming a completely new person.

When I first heard the formula, I was floored. I didn't believe it at first, but then I watched movie after movie and they all followed Michael's exact formula. Try it for yourself.

One of my favorite movies, *National Lampoon's Christmas Vacation,* even fits the mold. Clark Griswold is determined to create the perfect family Christmas. But the quest goes horribly and hysterically wrong. At the end, Clark creates an unforgettable family memory and learns that families don't need to be perfect, they just need to be together.

My guilty pleasure, the reality television show *The Bachelor,* also follows the formula. In it, the bachelor has one goal: to find his true love. Throughout the season, ridiculous drama ensues, and the bachelor isn't sure the process will work for him. Then he finds his true love and they live happily ever after. (For a month, at least!)

Bachelor fans love to watch him find his true love and witness his personal transformation as he faces his biggest fears.

What's funny is, although we know that this is the plot line and we *know* what the ending will be, we *still* follow the journey, season after season.

Now let me throw a wild and crazy concept at you. Your life is no different than the hero's two journeys. It is following the formula—you just probably didn't realize it until now.

If you decide to accept your mission as an Unstoppable Influencer, your outer journey will be the process you follow to fulfill your calling. The inner journey will be one of personal transformation, as you come into alignment with your true self and remove all the crap from your life that's been dimming your light. Super cool, right?

Here's the thing. The necessary and predictable part of BOTH journeys is challenge and struggle. Why? Well first, from the movie perspective, if Clark Griswold had said, "I want to have the perfect Griswold family Christmas," and then proceeded to Pinterest and Martha-Stewart the shit out of the holidays with his Leave-it-to-Beaver family, who would want to watch it? Not me.

More importantly, if Clark hadn't endured so many struggles, how could he ever truly appreciate his perfectly imperfect family?

As you embark upon the journey of Unstoppable Influence, you must anticipate that you will have times of struggle. It's part of the legacy you'll leave behind. When life gifts you lessons in the form of challenges, embrace them.

If everything always worked out perfectly, you would never grow. How could you? So welcome obstacles, and view them for what they are—opportunities for growth.

As you prepare to embark on your journey to Unstoppable Influence, be aware of the three hurdles that could trip you up if you aren't careful.

- ❖ Hurdle #1: Viewing an obstacle as a sign that you shouldn't be doing something
- ❖ Hurdle #2: Letting your Ego run the show
- ❖ Hurdle #3: Letting other people's Egos influence your life

Let's look at each of the hurdles and how to handle them when they appear.

Hurdle #1: Viewing an obstacle as a sign that you shouldn't be doing something

Far too many Influencers fall into the trap of thinking challenges are a sign from above that they shouldn't be doing something. I can't tell you the number of people I've worked with over the years who are ready to bail at the first sign of adversity.

Their logic goes something like this: "If I'm *supposed* to be doing X, then everything should flow easily, without any problems. After all, if God wants me to do this, He should give me smooth waters to get to my destination."

Seriously?

Have you *read* the Bible?! Who had smooth sailing in there? No one.

Do you think Daniel started questioning God down in the lion's den? How about Abraham's and Sarah's 100- and 90-year respective waits for their firstborn child? Did Jesus have smooth sailing in His life?

It doesn't take a biblical scholar to answer that—no way! If Daniel, Abraham, Sarah, and Jesus had to face adversity, so will you.

Adversity doesn't necessarily mean that you *shouldn't* be doing something. Occasionally, yes, it can mean that. However, only 20% of the time is it a sign that you should move to something else; 80% of the time, those struggles are really tools to assist in your growth.

You may be thinking, "If God wants me to do something, then why wouldn't He just allow me to reach my goal effortlessly?" The reason is that you must learn certain lessons so you can fulfill your purpose.

Case in point: I had to endure three years of law school, two grueling bar exams, and eight years of full-time law practice in order to figure out what I didn't want. If I hadn't, I wouldn't have been motivated or able to discover what I *did* want.

If we hadn't lost our business after 18 months of hard work, we wouldn't have embarked on our journey to build our own brand.

If I had been able to get pregnant immediately and hadn't battled infertility, depression, and grief, you wouldn't be reading these words right now.

If I hadn't endured the struggles and had just jumped ship at the first sign of adversity, Cristy would still be burning the midnight oil to make $30,000 per year, while her relationships continued to suffer. Heather wouldn't have launched her own coaching program, which is transforming lives. Angela would have kept her gift as a soul mentor on the shelf.

I had to struggle and face adversity to become an Unstoppable Influencer and to help others like you do the same.

Even more importantly, adversity and struggle practically force you to reconnect with your Source. Even the most anti-spiritual among us will fall to our knees in prayer in times of trial. When you feel helpless, you defer to the only One who you know can rise above.

When everything is going great, especially for long periods of time, you tend to get complacent. Your Ego (Hurdle #2) takes control and says, "I'm good. I've got this."

In those moments, you disconnect from your Source. When you do so, slowly but surely, fear, worry, and anxiety begin to take hold. When those feelings take over, you become further disconnected, and the downward spiral continues.

So when adversity appears, here's what you need to do.

1. First, don't view it as a dead end, view it as an on-ramp to your personal Inspiration Superhighway.
2. Next, thank God for the lessons being gifted to you at that moment.
3. Then ask Him to reveal the alternative routes for you to take.
4. When the resources and tools are revealed, take action.
5. Finally, when you've overcome the hurdle, reflect on the lessons and consider how you can use them to help others.

Hurdle #2: Letting your Ego run the show

The Ego is a nasty little bugger that's damn good at pretending to be your savior, when it's really nothing more than a saboteur. Ken Blanchard likes to say that "Ego stands for *edging God out.*" I agree.

You may have heard about the Ego back in Psychology class. That's not what I'm referring to. I'm also not talking about having *an ego*, meaning being conceited or vain.

The Ego I'm talking about is the loudmouth in your head that's constantly blabbing. She's the absolute *worst* right before you go to sleep—tormenting you with the tasks you didn't get done that day and the chores that need to be done the next day. While she's at it, your Ego will give you a list of shit to worry about that, quite frankly, will probably never happen.

Your Ego is also the asshole that talks you OUT of pursuing your passions and sharing your gifts. In fact, she's probably telling you right now that this whole Unstoppable Influence thing is BS, and that it's for other people, not you.

Your Ego is 100% responsible for shoving you into the security of your comfort zone and pouring concrete in there to try to prevent you from leaving. She does that masterfully by triggering the gag reflex when you even allow yourself to *think* of leaving your comfort zone.

You know *exactly* who I'm talking about.

Guess what? That bitch isn't real. She's imaginary and nothing but a fleeting thought. You know what IS real? Your Creator and your soul. They're real. Energy is real. Science proves it.

To this very day, the best scientists in the world *still* can't figure out where the very first particle came from. God is real—you may just use a different name for Him/Her/It.

So if God is real, and your Ego isn't—who do you want to listen to? Because you've been given free will, you can allow your Ego to run the show, although you really shouldn't.

Do you want to know what comes from your Source? Love, joy, compassion, light, and generosity.

What does your Ego bring to the party? Fear, scarcity, anxiety, worry, blame, shame, and anger. Ugh. No thank you!

Sadly, most people allow their Egos to run their lives. It's why record numbers of people are struggling with depression, alcoholism, and drug abuse. They have consciously or subconsciously distanced themselves from their Source of goodness, light, and love. As a result, they live in constant fear, anger, worry, blame, and shame.

Over the past seven years, I've seen numerous Influencers sidelined because of their Egos. As a coach, it pains me to watch this happen.

When I first started coaching, I had the privilege of meeting a young Influencer named Michael. He was determined to start his own business and proudly declared that he'd never receive a W–2 form (for employees) because he would never work for anyone else. Michael wanted to be his own boss.

I became Michael's mentor, and together we created an incredible personal brand and business for him. He was winning sales awards in the company he promoted, had his own clients, and was regularly generating leads and sales.

Then one day, his primary online lead source dried up. No matter how hard he tried, he couldn't generate leads the way he had before.

Michael first looked to other avenues, including a completely new business. However, the challenges overcame him and he eventually quit.

Michael went and got a "real" job, and received the dreaded W–2 form. One day, he wrote to tell me that thanks to his job, he'd paid off all his debt. I could tell he was excited. Paying off his business credit card debt was one thing Michael had always spoken about.

As soon as I heard that, though, I knew his Ego was the likely culprit behind the decision to quit his business and give up on his entrepreneurial dreams.

Instead of connecting to his Source and embarking on the Inspiration Superhighway, Michael was allowing his Ego to run the show. His Ego made statements like:

> "You'll never make enough money to pay off your credit card debt."

> "Debt is irresponsible—you may go bankrupt and people will think poorly of you."

> "Everyone else has a job, so you need one too."

As I read and reread Michael's text, I thought, "That's great— you're debt-free! But guess what? Your Ego will never allow you to enjoy the peace you think will come from that. Never. It won't be long before your Ego introduces another thing to worry about that will distract you from your true purpose."

You see, when you're connected to your Source, there's no room for Ego. Ego doesn't like that. Your Ego is bossy and likes to be in charge. So it's going to keep you as far away as possible from connecting to your Source.

Sneaky little bugger, isn't it?

The good news is that once you're *aware* that your Ego is a fraud, you can refocus your attention on connecting to your Source, from whom all blessings flow.

Now you may be wondering if Michael's a lost cause. No way. There will come a day when he'll reconnect with his purpose. I don't know the circumstances that will cause him to reconnect, but the day *will* come.

You see, Michael has Influencer DNA, just like you and me. Free will allows him to distance himself from his calling, but eventually the pull to fulfill his purpose will become so strong, he'll reengage in his work.

Right now, Michael is collecting valuable lessons, just like I did for several years, but his time to shine will come.

Hurdle #3: Letting other people's Egos influence your life

As if it isn't hard enough to battle your own damn Ego, as an Unstoppable Influencer, you'll have to put up with *other* people's Egos too. We'll call them OPE for short. Other people's Egos are strong and can be manipulative. They can cause the most Unstoppable Influencer to be stuck on the side of the road for years or even decades because of their own limiting beliefs.

Not only does your own Ego disguise itself as a savior, it does the same in other people's lives too. This means that when people deliver messages to you from their Egos, they'll preface them with comments like…

> "I'm only telling you this for your own good."

> "I love/care about you, so I need to share this with you."

> "I'm worried about you. I don't want anything bad to happen to you."

My own parents have made statements like this to me over the years. As children, we view our parents as superheroes. They're older and wiser. They have more life experience. So they *must* have all the answers, right?

Nope. They're perfectly imperfect. Just. Like. Us.

It wasn't until I became a mom that I discovered parents really *don't* have all the answers.

When the nurse placed my daughter in my arms for the first time, I couldn't help but think, *What the hell am I supposed to do now? I'm not prepared for this!*

Truth is, I wasn't prepared, but I learned as I went along. I didn't have all the answers from the start. Neither did my parents, even though I thought they did.

I took what my parents told me as gospel, and never questioned them. After all, they were my parents. They loved me and wanted to protect me. They only wanted what was best for me, right? Yes, but there was a catch.

My parents *did* and still *do* want the very best for me. They still try to protect me because they want me to have an amazing experience filled with the best life has to offer, while minimizing my pain.

I know they feel this way, because I feel the same way about my daughter. *But* (as one of my elementary school teachers used to say, "It's a really BIG BUT"), they have bossy Egos too.

Their Egos dump the same worries, anxieties, fear, doubt, shame, and guilt on them as mine dumps on me. In fact, the Ego works in overdrive when it comes to children. Those feelings are exponentially larger when it comes to those you love. So you feel *compelled* to save your loved ones from heartache and disappointment. You can't help yourself—you want to protect your own.

But protect them from what?

That's the thing. The Ego frequently creates much ado about nothing.

The reality is, I can't put my child into a bubble, any more than my parents could have put me into one. Children must experience life—the good and the bad. They must have opportunities to learn the lessons they're here to learn, so they can grow into the people they were meant to be, and discover their own Truth.

We'll dive more into the Ego in later chapters, but the important lesson to take from this is, when you hear those well-meaning statements from other people, there's a good chance they're coming from their Egos. Although you can't control other people's Egos, you *can* control how you react to them.

Certainly, God speaks to us through others. However, you have to know where the message is coming from. This is where you'll need to sharpen your skills of discernment.

EQUIPPING YOURSELF WITH THE TOOL OF DISCERNMENT

Since there are *two* voices competing for your attention, you must be able to distinguish where the voice is coming from— Ego or Source (Truth).

The easiest way to determine this is to meditate or pray. Don't be shy. Ask for signs to confirm whether the statements shared with you are Truth or Ego.

For me, one surefire sign that something is true is when I get goosebumps seemingly out of nowhere. It may seem odd, but that's just what I experience.

Another way I distinguish between the two is looking at the emotions attached to the thought. If it's fear, blame, shame, anxiety, or guilt, then I know it's Ego based. If the emotion attached is love, joy, compassion, light, or generosity, then it's from God.

You may have your own tool of discernment. The most important thing is that you recognize the existence of the two voices and then distinguish between them. Awareness is a powerful tool, and when equipped with discernment, you can clear any hurdle that comes your way.

LET'S REVIEW

❖ Your journey of Unstoppable Influence is two-fold. You'll embark on the outer journey of spreading your message to the world. You'll also embark on the inner journey of personal transformation and growth.

❖ There will be challenges along your path. You will struggle at times. You are being gifted lessons during those times, so embrace them. Remember that you can't grow without adversity.

❖ Encountering adversity doesn't necessarily mean you *shouldn't* be doing something. Sometimes it's a sign to move on to something else. But more often, it's an opportunity for growth.

❖ There are two voices competing for your attention. The first is your Ego, and it's a jerk. The other is your Source, from whom all goodness and blessings flow. Equip yourself with the tools necessary to discern between the two. Listen to and trust your Source. It will never steer you wrong.

❖ Your loved ones aren't perfect. Many of their warnings and concerns stem from their own bossy Egos. Use good judgment before acting upon their counsel.

❖ Other people's Egos can cause an Unstoppable Influencer like you to be sidelined for years, but they can't derail you permanently. Your purpose is always there, and you'll eventually feel the nudge to reconnect with it.

TAKE ACTION NOW

1. Before you go to bed at night and before you wake up in the morning, take time to clear your mind of your Ego's chatter and listen for the still inner voice of your Source. This practice takes time, so commit to at least five minutes each session.

2. Before making any decisions, ask yourself, "Is this choice being guided by my Source or by my Ego?" This will help you strengthen your discernment muscle. You can ask God three separate times to hear the answer. This is part of the Universal Law of Threes. The first time, your Ego usually gets in the way; the second time is usually correct; and the third time will give you the confirmation you seek.

3. Everyone has thoughts they replay over and over again in their minds. What are some potentially unproductive thoughts you repeat to yourself? List them and categorize them as either Ego or Truth.

CHAPTER 8

THE BUSY BEE TRAP

Either you run the day or the day runs you.

~ Jim Rohn

OMG, if I had a penny for every time I asked someone how they've been doing and they respond, "Busy," I'd give Bill Gates a run for his money.

Holy shit, y'all! Since when did being busy become some sort of badge of honor?

Don't get me wrong, I'm guilty as sin of giving the same response. But now that I recognize what a crappy response that is, I cringe whenever I hear it.

Here's the thing: Busy-ness is NOT a virtue.

Let me repeat that. Busy-ness is NOT a virtue, my friend. It's a vice. Shocking, I know, but stick with me on this one.

The reason we cling to this phrase is that we want people to see that our lives are full. We seem important because we're *so* busy.

Your life IS full. The problem is that it's filled with a bunch of shit that doesn't matter, like jobs and tasks that don't fulfill you or bring you joy.

Humor me for a second and dissect last week, for example. How much of your time was spent doing mindless work that didn't bring you any joy or fulfillment?

Dishes? Yard work? Paying bills? Grocery shopping? Laundry? Errands?

Think about how you felt last week. Exhausted? Stressed? If you're like most people, the answer is probably yes.

As a working mom, I usually only get peace and quiet when I'm in the shower. Even then, there's no guarantee I won't hear "Mommy? Mommy? MOOOMMMYYY" right outside the door.

I get it. It's tough.

Here's the thing, though. If you're ALWAYS in a state of "rush, rush, rush" and you never have time to just sit still, just "be," and connect to God, then you're never going to allow yourself the opportunity to hop on the Inspiration Superhighway and connect to your Truth.

Your Truth is a quiet voice. It's quite the contrast to your loud Ego or your spouse, kids, clients, or parents, who are clamoring for your attention at any given moment.

To connect with God and your Truth, you need some time away from all the noise to sit, stand, or lie down, and just be still and listen.

Now I know what you're probably thinking, because I thought this was all BS too when I first heard it.

"I don't have TIME to sit and *just listen*, because I've got work to do."

I get it. I've got a stack of massage gift cards waiting to be used during my "off" time. But here's the thing—the time will *never* appear spontaneously. You'll have to *make* the time.

There will never be a time when your to-do list items have all been checked off. There will always be another list. As someone once told me, "Your inbox will *never* be empty." So don't stress yourself out trying to keep it empty.

In these moments of the day-to-day working-mom grind, I'm reminded of the story of Sisyphus.

In Greek mythology, Sisyphus was a king who was punished for his self-aggrandizing craftiness and deceitfulness. His punishment was to roll an immense boulder up a hill only to watch it roll back down, so he would again have to push it up the hill, only to watch it roll back down again.

He was punished by having to endure this task for all of eternity. That's where we get the phrase a Sisyphean task. It's one that's laborious and never-ending. Sound familiar?

So if you're never going to get to the end of your to-do list, you'll just have to find another way to make time for God.

NATURE ABHORS A VACUUM

Another lesson I've learned over the years is that nature abhors a vacuum. If there is an empty slot in our calendar, we'll fill it up with something. It's how we operate, right?

So you will have to make time for yourself. If this concept sounds too "luxurious" and you're having a hard time doing it for yourself, then rephrase it as making time for God.

We all come from one Source. We all have a part of this Source within us, so you need to regularly connect with it if you're going to live life in alignment with your purpose.

To fulfill your mission as an Unstoppable Influencer, you absolutely *must* make time for your Source. It's non-negotiable.

There's a specific reason that I promise to help people boost their income and influence *without working longer hours*. It's not that I want my clients to become lazy. It's because relationships are important. Self-care is important.

It's during these times when we're *not* at work that we have the opportunity to "plug in" to our Source and recharge our physical, emotional, and spiritual batteries.

I've learned that having time to recharge is critical, no matter how much you love what you do. *Especially* if you love what you do.

I absolutely adore inspiring others and working with my clients. Truly. I get tremendous joy and fulfillment when I'm working with and serving others. But when I give, give, give, my battery gets depleted.

I'm not superhuman, and neither are you. We all have limits.

When I neglect self-care, I get sick far more often. I battle fatigue. I begin eating more junk food. It turns into a vicious cycle. I eventually lose all inspiration and end up completely drained, physically and mentally, for weeks.

That's not okay. Neglecting yourself and time with God is not the kind of behavior that helps you become Unstoppable. In fact, it does just the opposite.

"I'M TOO HIGH-STRUNG. HOW CAN I SIT STILL?"

If that's what you're saying right now, I know EXACTLY how you feel. I'm the person who damn near got kicked out of yoga class in Dallas. I've also been a nightmare client for anyone giving me a facial, massage, or any other spa service. I can't sit still.

When people told me I needed to "relax and just be," I wanted to smack 'em! In fact, the concept of sitting still irritated me for years. I was convinced that I was just not wired for meditation and other quiet activities.

After I hit rock bottom, I became willing to rethink every aspect of how I lived my life—even if it meant doing some meditation.

Admittedly, I'm far from mastering the meditation game. I think it's because I've got an especially chatty Ego that just won't shut up. Just quieting my mind to where there's nothing flashing through it is a Herculean task.

Now though, instead of trying to avoid the challenge, I'm facing it head-on. Having time to simply sit still and listen has profoundly changed my life for the better. I'm more inspired.

I'm more energized. I'm a better mother, wife, friend, daughter, and coach.

If meditation can work for me, it can certainly work for you too. If you're high-strung like me, it won't be easy at first. But you must block out the time on your calendar and just do it.

Here are three ways I started to ease myself into the process of meditation.

1. Set a timer for 10 minutes. Lie down on your bed and close your eyes. Imagine the color white. That's it. Nothing else. Just the color white. Meditation requires practice. Just like toning a muscle, you'll have to build up to it. Consistency is key.

2. Another way that I started forcing myself to sit still is by taking a warm bath with Epsom salt in it before I go to bed, at least three nights a week. I set my timer for at least 15 minutes, light some candles, turn on some meditation tunes, and add a few drops of essential oil to the water. Then I just relax.

3. The other method that works really well for me is listening to soothing music right before I go to bed.

I have these amazing headphones that are contained within a soft headband, with a cord in the back. I put the headband over my eyes, meditate, then just fall asleep.

They've worked wonders for me, and if you have a hyperactive mind like I do, this little gem coupled with a hypnosis track or meditation music can make a world of difference for you.

I've included a link to tools I use at Unstoppable Influence.com/store.

"WHAT AM I SUPPOSED TO DO WHEN I'M SITTING STILL?"

When you shut your mind off and just listen, you'll begin to discover the Truth of who you *really* are and your purpose (if you don't know what it is yet).

If you *do* know your purpose, you'll discover what you're supposed to do NEXT with your gifts. Who will you serve? How will you serve?

Remember that there are competing voices. So you'll want to use the tool of discernment to ensure that the voice you're listening to is the one from your Source, not your Ego.

The point of this quiet time is *not* to give God a laundry list of complaints and desires. You can save that for other quiet times. During your meditation time, the purpose is to just be still and listen.

It may surprise you to know that even someone like me has been able to remain in this inspiration-gathering state for way longer than 15 minutes.

In fact, every time I opened my laptop to write this book, I was in an inspiration state. Truly.

Every chapter was written the same way. I opened a blank page, closed my eyes, and began typing. The words just flowed through me.

I'm nothing special. You have the same ability within you. All it takes is linking up to your Source and just listening.

One last note: When you feel more inspired, you will be more productive. Working less can actually help your business and relationships thrive.

By the way, if you're itching to learn how to boost your influence and income without longer hours, we'll get there, I promise. There are just a few more concepts you need to know first.

LET'S REVIEW

- ❖ Being busy isn't a virtue; it's a vice.
- ❖ Your to-do list will never be completely done, so block out time to just sit still and listen.
- ❖ Although you do have some awesome superpowers, you're not invincible. You must carve out non-negotiable time for self-care to recharge your mental, physical, and spiritual batteries.
- ❖ Even the most high-strung people are capable of meditating successfully.
- ❖ If you never make time to simply sit still and connect with God, you'll deprive yourself of the opportunity to hop on the Inspiration Superhighway and connect to your Truth.
- ❖ When you shut your mind off and just listen, you'll begin to discover the Truth of who you *really* are and how to use your gifts for the greatest good.
- ❖ Less is more when it comes to working in your business. Your business should be structured in a way that

you're able to maximize your income without working long hours.

TAKE ACTION NOW

1. Using the template in the *Unstoppable Influence Companion Workbook*, map out your week. How are you spending your time? Are you taking care of yourself at least once a week?

2. Set aside 15 minutes every day for the next week to meditate.

3. Soak in a warm Epsom-salt bath and listen to relaxing music for 15–20 minutes at least once this week. Check out the Unstoppable Influence Store for some of my favorites: UnstoppableInfluence.com/store.

CHAPTER 9

WHAT DO YOU REALLY WANT?

*You are never too old to set another goal
or to dream a new dream.*

~ C.S. Lewis

You now know what it means to be an Unstoppable Influencer and some of the challenges you'll face along the way.

But where are you headed?

The answer really depends on this one concept: your Truth.

Now before you can get to your Truth, you'll have to wade through a *ton* of BS. Seriously. Tons.

Why?

To get to your Truth, you must answer this question:

Who am I without limitations?

Well, damn, limitations are *everywhere*! You put them on yourself and your family, friends pile 'em on, and then society adds in more for good measure. In fact, limitations affect every single decision you make—what car to drive, which home to buy, what school your children attend, where you work, how much you charge, who you marry—the list goes on and on.

I know that asking you to imagine a life without limitations is a tall order. But it's surprisingly easy when you understand what they are.

Obviously, you're not going to have a life without any limitations, and that's not the point. The point is to recognize the ones that cause you to make incorrect assumptions about *who you are* and *what you're capable of*. Then, for a *brief* moment, release those limitations so you can take a peek at your Truth.

Why you are here? Who can you serve? How can you serve? It's a preview to the movie of a life of authenticity, where you are living your Truth.

The first step is to recognize the limitations in your life. So for the purpose of this next exercise, you must assume the following:

* You have access to all the *knowledge* in the world.
* You have all the *support* in the world, from every single person.
* You have all the *money* in the world.
* You have all the *confidence* in the world.
* You have all the *resources* in the world.
* You *look the way you want to look.*
* You're the *age* you want to be, and you're in *perfect health.*

- You're in the *perfect relationship* (or you're single if that's more your jam).
- You *live where you want to live.*
- You're *incapable of failure.*

Phew! Okay, now I want you to grab a pen and the *Companion Workbook*. Put on some relaxing music, shut the door, and close your eyes.

I want you to *feel* what it feels like to have *everything* I just mentioned. It should feel freeing—you're operating without limitations!

Now I want you to stay in that place and write for at least 15 minutes, but longer if the Spirit moves you, to answer the question:

Who am I without limitations?

Go on and do it now.

Here's just a tiny part of what I wrote.

> Natasha Nassar Hazlett is a *New York Times* best-selling author, speaker, thought leader, and mentor to millions.

When I looked at it, I couldn't believe it. That was *me*? That was my *Truth*?

Then again, I *could* believe it. And do you know what? I did believe it (and still do). The words flowed so effortlessly from my pen that I knew it was my Truth.

In that moment, as I read and reread the words on the page, I thought, *This is who I am.* Once I knew who I really was, I had no choice *but* to operate in alignment with my Truth. Anything less than that would be inauthentic.

The same will happen for you when you do this exercise. Once you have a glimpse of who you *really* are and the potential that exists within you, there's simply no turning back.

How do I know?

The people I've met who are *truly* Unstoppable Influencers are the *most* authentic individuals I know. They operate with a higher level of integrity than most.

This is why, once you discover your Truth (who you are without limitations), you can't put the toothpaste back in the tube. It's out there, and it's difficult to live out of alignment with your Truth. Fair warning though—moving from *knowing* your Truth to stepping in and living it will require you to step outside your comfort zone.

You can run. You can hide. You can try your mightiest to avoid your Truth. But it will never *feel* right. It will keep drawing you in, and eventually you'll have no choice but to begin living in alignment with your Truth.

Some of you may be wondering, "Is she *really* talking to *me*?" Yes. I'm writing this book for those with the Influencer DNA. Of course, you're all in different stages of your respective journeys. Some are just exploring or stepping into your purpose, others may have been living and walking in their Truth for decades.

Regardless of where you are, if you're reading this right now, you're really, truly, authentically an Influencer. Yay!

Now, it's time to set some goals (or intentions) for your journey over the next few years. Sure, you could do five- or ten-year goals, but for the purpose of getting you into the right frame of mind, I want you to focus on the next three years.

Knowing now *who you really are...*

Where do you want to be on this date, three years from now?

Seems like a fairly straightforward question, but don't make the mistake of setting goals or intentions you think are realistic or safe. Too many people set goals based upon what's doable, so you focus on *how* you can make it happen instead of *what* you really, truly want.

When you focus on the *how*, you mess it all up. Why?

Because when you're focused on the *how*, you're pulling God out of the game, and putting Him on the bench. You're *not* making room for miracles. That sucks, because miracles are awesome! I mean, have you ever heard anyone say, "I experienced a miracle this morning and it totally sucked!" Yeah, I didn't think so.

Miracles are specially crafted gifts from God just for you, and who doesn't like gifts?

I have to say that as an attorney, I had a hard time getting out of the "how can I make this happen" mindset when setting goals. It frustrated the hell out of poor Rich. He was an avid student of personal development from a very young age. He's listened to thousands of hours of training on goal setting and the power of the mind. As a result, he knew that we should be setting goals based on *what* we really want, instead of settling for reasonable goals based on what we *think* we can accomplish based on our current situation.

So when it came time to set our business goals, Rich would come in with a huge goal, and I would always pooh-pooh it. I would roll my eyes and then give him my lawyerly analysis of why it would never happen.

I would then supply a reasonable goal, and he would get frustrated because I was just settling. I'll admit that on this particular issue, Rich was right and I was wrong. (See that, Rich, it's in black and white and on record!)

I tell that story for the benefit of you logical, analytical types. I know *exactly* how you feel. While I empathize, I'll also say that's the *wrong* way to set your goals. You've got to make room for miracles.

So your next assignment is to decide what you really want.

The key to getting everything you want over the next three years, and quite frankly throughout your life, is simple.

Decide what you really, truly want, then ask for it.

There are two super important concepts within this strategy, and both must be mastered as an Unstoppable Influencer.

The first step is to play around with the ideas of what you really want.

It can be really hard, but for the purpose of this next exercise, you'll need to once again release all the limitations from your conscious mind.

Then grab your pen, download the Universe Superstore Claim Form at UnstoppableInfluence.com/claim, then answer this question:

What do I have in my life because I face no limitations?

Close your eyes and return to a state of mind where money flows freely. All the resources you need are abundant. You're in a place of no judgment.

Imagine yourself in the Universe Superstore, with NO spending limit.

No one says no. There's nothing right or wrong in your shopping basket (which keeps expanding, by the way). You can literally have whatever you want.

What's going in your cart?

An awesome soulmate? That Range Rover Sport? A five-thousand-square-foot house?

Maybe there's a pool? Children? Good health? Millions of dollars in the bank?

Debts paid in full? Vacations four times a year? Private school for your kids? Monthly massages?

What do you *want* from the Universe Superstore?

Once you've taken at least 15 minutes to create your Universe Shopping List, read through it and *decide* which of those items you really want in the next three years.

The word DECIDE is powerful and important. It comes from the Latin word *decidere*, which translates as "to cut off."

When you truly *decide*, you're literally cutting off all other options. There is no retreat. Then after you decide what you really want, **ask for it**.

God wants you to have what your heart desires and what's good for you and your journey. How do I know that? It says so throughout the Bible—no fewer than 10 times.

The most popular verse is:

> Ask and it will be given to you; seek and you will find; knock and the door will be opened to you. For everyone who asks receives; the one who seeks finds; and to the one who knocks, the door will be opened. Matthew 7:7-8 (NIV)

How much clearer could it be?

If the Bible isn't your thing, then cool—try the Law of Attraction on for size. It basically says that energy attracts like energy. Positive energy attracts positive experiences. Negative energy attracts negative experiences.

Decide what you want, and you can attract it into your life.

Note that I didn't say all you need to do is "ask and then figure out how it's going to happen."

Just ask.

If in your prayers tonight you ask God to move a mountain for you, you may wake up in the morning to see that the mountain is gone. But you might just wake up and find a shovel in your hand! Either way, go to work on what's next.

Be vigilant and watch for the answers to come into your life.

It may be through reading something in a book, hearing something a friend says, or meeting a person who can help you. Sometimes it's the words of a song or even a small voice that gives you an answer while you're in the shower.

Answers come in many different ways, but they always come. Always.

The answers may not be what you want or expect, and they may not come on your timeline. But they always arrive in perfect, divine timing.

Now if you do what I used to do, though, you may miss the answers. I used to ask, then tie myself up in knots trying to figure out the "how." Or worse, I would try to figure out the "how" first, and if I couldn't, I wouldn't even ask for it.

If that's you—stop it!

Just ask for what you truly want.

Again, this is *completely* different from asking for what you *think* you can get. What you think you can get is (99.99% of the time) way less than what you truly want. If you're like me, you're so damn used to settling for less that you ask for the bare minimum. Not surprisingly, that's all you get.

Instead, ask for whatever it is that you *really, truly* want. Ask for the whole damn enchilada. Don't be bashful, because there's plenty for everyone.

Once when I was teaching this concept on a Facebook Live video, Sarah, a friend I hadn't spoken with in nearly 10 years, sent me a message and told me how hectic her life was.

She and her husband lived apart. They both had good jobs, but although they had tried, they hadn't found suitable jobs in the same state yet.

Sarah said that what she really wanted was for them to both move back home to be closer to family. So I asked her, "Why not just move there?" She said they'd been looking for jobs for a couple of years, but no viable opportunities existed.

My response was simple: "I have complete confidence that the moment you decide to make the move, the right opportunities will open up. You just have to quit waffling and commit. You will find jobs."

Five weeks later, Sarah sent me this message.

> Just an FYI on what's going on with us. You were right. Once I said it out loud, it started changing. I wanted to move back home. Like magic, an awesome federal job opened up,

[and my husband] applied, interviewed, and negotiated an offer. Boom! All I had to do was say it out loud. "Here's what I want!" And it started to happen.

The strategies I'm sharing with you *really* work!

Here's what I love most about the concept of deciding what you want and then getting it—you don't have to know *how* or *why* it works. I mean, do you know how a light bulb works? I sure as hell don't.

Does that prevent you from having confidence that the light will come on when you flip the switch?

Nope. You don't have to understand how or why something works for it to work. The same thing goes for this whole deciding what you want and asking for it gig. You don't have to understand how, just have faith that it will.

You may be thinking, "Natasha, this Universe Superstore concept sounds cool and all, but how in the hell does it relate to being an Unstoppable Influencer?"

If Unstoppable Influence was a car, the concept you've just learned is the fuel. It helps you get where you're going.

Here's why: Once you *decide* to answer the call to become an Unstoppable Influencer, you'll need to ask for the resources necessary to fulfill your mission.

To unleash your influence and light in the world, you'll need to have all the necessary resources at your disposal.

That's going to cost money, because that's how we operate here in the physical world. So you need to *ask* for the resources, teachers, and mentors. *Ask* for the money from God. *Ask* for the money from your clients and customers by charging what you're worth.

Remember, God helps those who help themselves.

Sarah boldly declared what she had decided to do—move back to her home state with her husband. Afterward, she didn't just sit on her ass and wait for something to happen. She started looking for jobs. A job then appeared. Very quickly, I might add.

This reminds me of the story of two farmers from the movie *Facing Giants*.

Both farmers desperately needed rain, and both prayed for rain. But only one of them went out and prepared his fields to receive it. He plowed the land and planted the seeds. When God eventually sent the rain, who reaped the harvest? The one who prepared his field, of course.

Which one do you think trusted God to send the rain? The one who prepared his fields for it!

Faith isn't just a noun. It's also a verb. Having faith and trusting God doesn't mean you should sit on your duff waiting for something to happen. You must get busy doing what needs to be done, so you can receive abundantly when God delivers what you ask for.

If you ask for the clients you're meant to serve, start building a business to serve them and charge appropriately (Chapter 18). You'll find that the necessary resources will come to you.

Although you may not be influencing thousands or millions currently, as an Unstoppable Influencer, you must prepare yourself to spread your message to your soon-to-be audience.

Cristy was most certainly the farmer who prepared for the rain. Although she was only making $30,000 a year when we first started working together, I was very up-front about what I felt it would take monetarily to get her message out on the big stage.

She was fully committed to stepping into her role as an Unstoppable Influencer. She decided that this was her intended path. Cristy asked for the resources she needed, then immediately did whatever it took to get them. One of those action steps included taking out a loan to front the expenses.

In doing so, she was preparing her fields for rain.

In less than a year, Cristy had earned enough to pay the entire loan back, pay off all her student loan debt, and buy her dream car!

You can get what you *really,* truly want in life. Just decide, ask, and prepare to receive.

LET'S REVIEW

* Take time to discover your Truth. Who are you without limitation?
* Once you decide what you want, *ask* for it. Don't be shy. Ask for the resources you need to unleash your influence in the world.

❖ After you ask for what you want, begin to prepare your fields for rain.

❖ Answers come in many different forms, *but they always come*. Remember that divine timing is perfect timing. Trust in that.

TAKE ACTION NOW

1. Complete the exercises discussed in this chapter in the *Companion Workbook* If you haven't done so already, you can download your digital copy of the *Companion Workbook* for FREE at UnstoppableInfluence.com/gift

2. Decide what you *really* and truly want out of life. Don't just settle for what you think you can get. Download your Universe Superstore Claim Form at UnstoppableInfluence.com/claim and start writing your list. Have fun!

3. Once you've decided what you want, *ask* for it, and then do the prep work necessary to receive it.

CHAPTER 10

DISCOVERING YOUR PURPOSE

*The creation of a thousand forests
is in one acorn.*

-- Ralph Waldo Emerson

Your light existed from the moment you were born.

Free will allows you to dim or brighten, hide or share your light, but it can never be extinguished. Your gift lies within your light. Your life's purpose is tied to that gift.

Some discover their gift and purpose at a young age, but many won't fully discover it until later in life. That's okay, because divine timing is perfect.

From a fairly young age, I knew I had been given the gift of leadership. It was something I could use to inspire and serve others.

However, it wasn't until I was 32 that I knew my calling. Receiving it was surreal.

I was reading a devotional called *Jesus Calling*. My sister-in-law, Kendra, had given me the book after my miscarriage, and I had tossed it into the nightstand because to be honest, I was really pissed off at Jesus at the time. He didn't give me a child, which is what I wanted, so I had no interest in having Him "call" me about *anything*.

Nearly a year later, I felt a nudge to pick up that book, so I started reading it every morning. Every message seemed to correlate to what was going on at that precise moment in my life.

THE RADICAL CALL

One December morning, I picked up my devotional and felt compelled to read the entry for a random day. As I read, a message was placed on my heart.

I wish I could explain it better, because it wasn't an audible or visual message. It was a silent one that led me to knowing the time had come to quit my job at the law firm so I could help entrepreneurs full-time.

I say my calling was surreal because Heaven knows (literally) that I wasn't inclined to go off half-cocked and quit my plush lawyer gig. I mean *everyone* knows that's *completely* irresponsible, right? I knew better than that!

However, in that moment, I was simply receiving information and not judging it. My client, Melissa, dubbed this phenomenon a "download."

It all happened so fast. In an instant, I "heard" everything, processed it, and comprehended it within the depths of my soul. A warm rush came over me as the incident unfolded, followed by goosebumps. Then it was gone.

What the hell just happened? I thought.

I ran out to tell Rich. "You won't believe this, but I *think* I got my calling!"

I'm pretty certain he thought I was crazy at first, but when I recounted the whole experience, he knew that this wasn't some harebrained story I'd invented.

He knew that I'd never insist on quitting my job because it wasn't like me.

This calling thing was *real.*

Let me tell you—just because you receive a calling doesn't mean you really *get* it. In fact, it wasn't until five and a half years *later* that I fully understood my purpose.

I just knew I was supposed to work with entrepreneurs, and that entrepreneurs have a special calling from God because they serve others. That's what business is all about, right? So I knew that I would help others serve more, and serve better.

Most people think a calling seems cool and perhaps even noble. That may be true, but it doesn't mean that you won't have doubts about it. I had *plenty* of doubts—heaps of them, in fact.

That's okay. You're entitled to doubt. You're entitled to question. You're even entitled to say, "Screw it. I'm not doing it!"

Why?

Free will, baby.

But as I've said time and time again, you were created *on* purpose, *for* a purpose. So like it or not, at some point you'll reconnect and fulfill your calling. This is deep, I know. Stick with me though.

Let's go back to the doubt part, because it's really important. It's okay to doubt. The main reason we doubt, and the main reason *I* doubted, was that I felt unprepared for my calling.

FEELING UNPREPARED

I've since learned that God *always* calls the unprepared, and then guess what? He prepares them.

To overcome my own doubts, I asked God to reveal signs to prove that my calling was legit. He delivered.

First, business started really slowing down at the firm, which meant I was being underutilized. Meanwhile, my coaching practice was skyrocketing. I quickly realized I was actually *losing* money at work. So I knew it was time to resign.

Then, in preparation for my "quit date" of August 1, I picked up *48 Days to the Work You Love* by Dan Miller. I felt a nudge to count 48 days from that date, just for fun. And 48 days from June 14 was…August 1. Coincidence? I don't think so.

As my two-week notice deadline rapidly approached, I started freaking out.

> *What if this calling is just some BS I imagined?*
>
> *What if I fail?*
>
> *What if we go bankrupt?*

What will my parents think?

All those thoughts swirled through my head, and pretty soon I started thinking that God had accidentally called the wrong girl. Here was my small-minded justification—I'm not a good Christian. My sister-in-law, Kendra, is a deacon in the church. She leads Bible studies. I drink and swear and don't even attend church regularly. I mean heck, I don't know Ruth from Esther, so why would God call *me*?

STEPPING UP AND SAYING YES

As my anxiety ratcheted up, I attended church on July 7, *just in time* for a new sermon series entitled "Answering the Radical Call."

I'm not kidding. I couldn't make this up if I tried!

For four weeks, I learned about the *ordinary* people God called to do *extraordinary* jobs. It wasn't the ultra religious or the ultra rich that God called. He called *those* who felt unprepared, and then prepared them.

For example, there's Mary. She was a 15-year-old, poor teenage girl. God, through archangel Gabriel, called her to bear His son. She could have been stoned to death for being pregnant while unmarried. Yet she had said yes to the call, and Jesus Christ was born.

Or how about the disciples Simon Peter and Andrew? They were fishermen. Can you imagine it? A guy named Jesus came strolling along the docks as Simon Peter and Andrew were coming in after a long day of work. Jesus told them to put down their nets and "Follow me, I'll make you fishers of men." Matthew 4:19 (NIV)

What did they do? They followed. Note that they *didn't* say, "Hey, Jesus! Does this disciple gig come with benefits? Health insurance? How about sick days?"

Nope. The Bible says they simply put down their nets and followed Him.

Dang.

Those calls made mine look like seriously small potatoes. If those people had felt unprepared but *still* said yes, I had absolutely no excuse.

So I agreed to do the big, scary thing I was called to do. On faith and faith alone, I moved forward with the plan to quit my job.

THE BIG PLUNGE

On July 18, I walked into my boss's office, with sweaty palms and all, and told him I needed to resign.

Hours of reciting my "quit speech" didn't prepare me for his reaction. He said, "Well, I'm not inclined to accept your resignation."

What?! I hadn't practiced this scenario in the mirror!

My badass, entrepreneur-loving boss offered me an "of counsel" position with the firm. This meant that I could keep my office and assistant, set my own hours, and work as an independent contractor. It was the best of both worlds.

MAKE THE LEAP FIRST

There's a really big lesson in this story, and I want to make sure you caught it—I had to take the leap of faith *first*.

I didn't know that I would be offered the "of counsel" position. I was ready to answer the radical call 110% without a safety net.

The story doesn't end there, though. A few days later, a business colleague invited Rich and me to form a joint venture partnership to sell a high-ticket coaching program. Rich and I said yes to this timely opportunity. Coincidence? Of course not.

In fact, three days after I quit my job, we made $23,000 from that joint venture, which lessened the blow when I informed my dad that I had just quit my job.

This experience taught me a profound lesson: When you're called to serve, and you unequivocally accept, you *will* be given the tools and resources you need to succeed. The only catch is, you typically won't see the resources until *after* you say yes.

So just say yes, then watch as the necessary tools and resources appear in your life, almost like magic!

Another important lesson I learned was that just because you're answering a calling doesn't mean you're immune from disappointment and challenges. I'll admit, this one really surprised me.

I figured that if I was fulfilling my purpose, God would give me a clear path. I was wrong.

NAVIGATING THE ROCKY ROAD

As I mentioned earlier, eventually the fog of fear and self-doubt rolled in and overcame me. It dimmed my light, so few could see and experience it.

Before I knew it, my light had dimmed so much that I'd lost all inspiration and motivation. In that dark moment, I nearly abandoned my calling.

If you've experienced this or are currently experiencing a similar darkness, remember one thing—your light is *always* within you.

It may be buried deep beneath heaps of emotional baggage, but it's still there.

Your calling *will* come a-knockin' again, just like the annoying but charming dog or cat that always wants to sit in your lap. Your purpose is always there—like it or not.

After the fog lifted, I still wasn't 100% certain of where I was headed with my calling. I just knew my first step was to release the fat.

This would kick-start my reinvention and my journey of "unbecoming."

As I was nearing my goal weight, God placed a gentleman named Joseph in my life. He is a #1 best-selling Hay House author and Celebrity Hypnotherapist.

I must tell you that I never believed in hypnosis. In fact, I didn't think I could even *be* hypnotized. But as part of my reinvention, I committed to doing life *differently*. I wanted to try new experiences that the old me would have said "Hell no" to. Since the old Natasha would have said hypnosis was BS, I said *yes* to the special hypnosis track that Joseph had created for entrepreneurs.

I listened to it right before I went to sleep, and I tried to focus on every word. I kept fighting the urge to fall asleep, because I didn't really know Joseph at the time, and for all I knew, he could've hypnotized me to cluck like a damn chicken, or convince me to send him all my money. You can never be too careful, right?

I suppose I eventually drifted to sleep, because the next morning, I awoke feeling like a complete and total badass.

Could the hypnosis shtick work? I wondered.

I didn't know for sure, but I wanted to try it again, *just in case.* The next morning, I awoke feeling like a freaking superhero.

I know what you're thinking. "Holy shit! You mean hypnosis actually works?"

Yes.

I started working individually with Joseph, and through his training, I began to finally understand the difference between the conscious and subconscious mind. He opened my eyes to a world I never knew about (the subconscious mind) and the fact that there was still so much I didn't know about who I really was.

GETTING CLARITY

A few weeks later, at 4:30 a.m. to be exact, I suddenly awoke to understand what "awareness" was. That was a concept I'd heard people talking about for years, but I had written off as New Age mumbo jumbo. Turns out, I was experiencing yet another download.

In an instant, I understood the roles of our Egos, souls, energy, and many other deep concepts that I'd avoided learning about because I was worried they weren't in alignment with my Christian beliefs. (I was *totally* wrong about that, by the way.)

Days later, on a quest to have more out-of-the-box experiences, I hired one of my clients for an energy clearing.

I was coming in hot, y'all—I wanted to know *more, more, more*! What *else* had I been missing? I wanted to know everything! I was ready to discover who I really was.

A few months later, just before I started writing this book, the phrase "Unstoppable Influence" was placed on my heart, and I knew that THIS was the movement God was calling me to lead. But I still didn't fully understand what I was supposed to do with it.

I just knew it would be big.

By this time, I'd become accustomed to just letting shit go and allowing God to lead me. So I did.

He led me to the annual Sun Valley Wellness Festival to receive the answers I sought.

(Side note: I've said it before and I'll say it again. Divine timing is *everything*. Had I gone to the Wellness Festival one year earlier, I would've dubbed it a "Woo Woo Fest" and avoided it at all costs.)

However, this time I was open. At this event, I saw and felt so much light, love, and positive energy. It was inexplicable and truly transformational. For the first time, I felt like I truly knew who I was and what my purpose was here on Earth.

In Sun Valley, I discovered my role as a connector. My mission was to bring together and help train a dream team of entrepreneurs, who shine their light in the world by using their gifts to serve others.

As a member of the Unstoppable Influence movement, you're an important part of bringing light and love to this world through your special gifts by saying "Hell yeah!" to your calling, whatever it may be.

Hopefully, by sharing my journey to discovering my purpose, you're able to recognize your own calling. More importantly, by the end of this book, you'll have the tools you need to identify and clear away the emotional baggage that's been holding you back from finding and fulfilling your purpose.

The journey to finding and living your purpose is just that—a journey. You probably won't figure it out all at once, and that's all right. Just know this—the world needs YOU right now. So roll up your sleeves and let's get to work, okay?

LET'S REVIEW

❖ Your light and gift existed the moment you were born.

❖ Free will allows you to dim or brighten, hide or share your light.

❖ Within your light is your gift. Your purpose is tied to your giftedness.

❖ God *always* calls the unprepared, then prepares them.

❖ Give an unequivocal "Hell yes" to your call first, then watch the necessary tools and resources appear.

❖ Finding and living your purpose is a *journey*, not a destination.

❖ You probably won't figure out your purpose all at once, and that's okay.

TAKE ACTION NOW

1. Meditate or pray on what you've been called to do.

2. If you have a calling but haven't acted upon it, reflect on the reasons why. What mental garbage is preventing you from living your life's purpose?

3. Commit to participating in three experiences that have the potential to help you grow personally over the next three months. It may be getting a massage for the first time, skydiving, or something in between. Brownie points if the experience scares the daylights out of you!

4. Download the special Unstoppable Influence Hypnosis Track created by Joseph Clough at UnstoppableInfluence.com/hypnosis

CHAPTER 11

STEPPING OUT IN FAITH

*Everything you've ever wanted is
on the other side of fear.*

~ George Adair

I'll admit it. Sometimes I like to be a copycat—especially when it comes to imitating someone I admire, like my friend and client, Heather. Several years ago, she shared a tradition she and her three children have, which is to pick a theme word for the upcoming year. Together they research, discuss, and ponder the possibilities until they each settle upon one perfect word for the year.

This was such a badass and inspiring tradition that I *had* to follow suit. Admittedly, the first couple of years, the words I came up with were pretty lame. They weren't a reflection of my year at all.

In fact, my 2016 theme word was "focus." I wanted to focus on my business. That's what I felt I *should* do, but God clearly had other plans. Had I truly tapped into my Zone of Truth, I would have gotten my "real" word for the year: reinvention.

REVELATIONS

In early December, I started thinking long and hard about my theme word for 2017. I didn't want to screw it up like I had in previous years, so this time I prayed a lot about the right word.

Right on time, the word appeared plain as day in my mind—FAITH.

Faith? That seems like such a cliché word. Seriously, God, You couldn't have come up with something a little more novel?

The response I got was more of the same—faith.

Okay, so my 2017 theme word will be faith. But faith in what context? I wondered. *I'm already very spiritual. I pray daily. How much more faith do I need?*

"A lot more. You need to have *real* faith in Me again," came the response.

I got it.

Ouch.

Real faith requires a willingness to take action *even* when the outcome is uncertain.

If I was honest with myself, I had faith…*when it was convenient*. When someone *else* was sick. When I was praying for something small and doable. When I was planning to take an action that would have no major consequences if I failed. It was easy to say I had faith in those moments.

But what about the big moments? What about when I got the nudge to host an event four times larger than previous events? One that required me to front a ton of cash with no guarantee of a return on our investment?

What about when the idea was placed on our hearts to move away from home and start over again in a new city?

Or perhaps when I was given the idea to write this book, and I had to scrub my calendar clean for a month, and deal with the consequences of setting aside my other obligations to finish it?

Those were bigger moments of personal, financial, and professional risk. Those were situations that *truly* tested the bounds of my faith.

And let me tell you something: I was scared. I still get scared at times. But if there's one thing I know, it's this: To grow into the Unstoppable Influencer who I am meant to become, I *have* to step outside my comfort zone.

Likewise, you must take a leap of faith, knowing that God will provide what you need.

You will have to be prepared to fight the battle with your Ego to stay focused. That loud, obnoxious voice in your head will sound the alarm when you're about to step outside your comfort zone.

Remember, it's a false alarm that you must ignore.

The most *amazing* gifts are waiting for you. They're sitting right *outside* your comfort zone. You just need to step out in faith. This is how you'll grow and stretch your mind and your beliefs and, most importantly, live your life by design.

I know, I know. Playing outside your comfort zone is *scary as Hell*. Just thinking of taking that leap of faith may trigger a wave of nausea. It's okay. That's a good thing. It's what I call the Comfort Zone Check.

Get used to it. Embrace it. I've *never once* regretted stepping outside my comfort zone. Never. That's a pretty bold statement, but I mean it.

The reason I've never regretted it is that I know God always has my back. Always.

He always equips me with the tools and resources I need. They may not come as quickly as I would hope (like before making a leap of faith), but they always come on time.

I remember studying the *Essential 100* stories of the Bible. I read story after story about how God provided for those He called to step out in faith—especially the Israelites.

I'd finish one story about the amazing acts of love that God bestowed upon His people, and then the next story was about how they started grumbling and complaining, and questioning whether God would be there for them again.

I wanted to shout at my Bible, "Seriously, y'all?!? You know of the parting of the Red Sea and the manna coming down from Heaven, but you still question whether God will provide for you?"

And yet, if I'm 100% honest, during my own trials, I had similarly questioned whether God would be there for me when I took a particular leap of faith.

I was guilty of the same lack of faith as the Israelites. I had made $23,000 in a single day, just three days after leaving my full-time job. How much more proof did I need?

That's when I realized I had a lot of work to do to build up my faith muscle, so I ultimately embraced that word for the year.

I knew I'd be challenged to continually say *yes* in the midst of my fear when it came to leveling up and spreading my message in a massive way.

The reality is, though, that to truly become an *Unstoppable* Influencer, you must have *faith* in a power greater than yourself..

It doesn't matter what you call that power, only that you have faith in it, and that you know your Creator will provide what you need at the perfect time. To take it a step further, you're going to have to make room for miracles.

Cristy's story is a perfect example. As I sat in her office, I knew she was intended to be on the "big stage," and I told her as much.

Although she didn't know *how* it would happen, Cristy decided in that moment to just have faith.

She had faith that God had placed me in her life for a specific reason—to guide her to live up to her God-given potential. In that moment, she made room for miracles.

And miracles indeed came from left and right. Cristy found the help she needed from many different sources.

My favorite story, though, is about the day that Cristy's publisher called us and said, "You won't believe this, but Amy Collins (one of the top book-buying experts in the world) loves what Cristy's doing and wants to help us spread her message."

Let me explain the miracle in that. Apparently, the bookstore world is locked up tighter than Fort Knox. For stores like Barnes & Noble to carry your books, you need either a ginormous publishing house like Random House or a miracle.

Amy Collins was that miracle. She's overseen book distribution for the past 40 years. She has built close relationships with the book buyers for Target, Costco, Walmart, Barnes & Noble, and all the major grocery stores. Amy's help would practically ensure that Cristy's book would hit the best-seller lists and that she would end up on that big stage.

Cristy's publisher was surprised by the news and ecstatic. I was thrilled, of course, but not surprised in the least. Cristy had made room for miracles, and the miracles came on cue. Just as expected.

Cristy was walking in her Truth. She was ready to unleash her influence into the world, and she made the room necessary for miracles so her potential could be transformed into reality.

MIRACLES ARE EVERYWHERE

Miracles are available to you too!

You just have to accept that there's a good chance you won't see the provisions available until *after* you step out in faith, because after all, that's what faith is: *believing without seeing.*

So put faith in your toolbox and make room for miracles, because it will be instrumental in your journey to becoming a truly Unstoppable Influencer and living your life by design.

I'll end this chapter with one of my all-time favorite quotes.

Be bold and mighty forces will come to your aid.

~ Basil King

LET'S REVIEW

❖ Faith requires a willingness to take action, even when the outcome is uncertain.

❖ When you make a leap of faith, know that God will provide what you need.

❖ The most AMAZING gifts and lessons are waiting for you to grab them. They're sitting right outside your comfort zone.

❖ A Comfort Zone Check = nausea, butterflies, or an adrenaline rush.

❖ Faith is the most important tool you can possess as an Unstoppable Influencer.

TAKE ACTION NOW

1. Select a theme word for this year.

2. Commit to stepping out in faith at least once a month for three months. Write down one faith-building activity for each of the next three months and set deadlines. Complete each activity by the deadline and take notes about how they made you feel and the lessons you learned.

3. Commit to making room for miracles, then watch as they flow into your life. Keep a journal and record all the miracles as they occur. Each night, give thanks for your daily miracles.

CHAPTER 12

YOUR TIME IS NOW!

The journey of a thousand miles
begins with one step.

~ Lao Tzu

I'll admit that when it comes to timing, I struggle. I'm notoriously late everywhere I go. Always have been. It's an abysmal habit that I'm working to break. In fact, it's such a bad habit that some friends give me a fake time (30 minutes earlier), just so I'll show up on time.

I even remember a few times back in college when I had to call friends to let them know that I was actually *on time* so they could plan their schedules accordingly. Who does that? Me, that's who!

Although I'm habitually late, I'm also extremely impatient. Ironic, isn't it?

I *hate* waiting. Especially when I'm waiting for something I really want. So you can imagine the frustration I felt when I had to wait until I was 26 to meet my future husband. All my friends were married and starting families, and I was still waiting for the right guy to show up.

Once I met Rich, I quickly realized he was "the one." So I switched from waiting for my soulmate to show up to waiting for him to propose. Nearly two years later, Rich proposed, and nine months after that we got married.

Rich and I both couldn't wait to be parents. However, instead of the eagerly anticipated "honeymoon baby," we faced disappointment after disappointment. The wait was excruciating. I cannot even begin to tell you the number of nights I cried myself to sleep during the Great Big Wait.

In fact, the more time that passed, the angrier I was with God for not giving me what I wanted, right when I wanted it.

"It's not FAIR!" I shouted one day in the car, with tears streaming down my cheeks.

"What did I do to deserve this kind of heartache? Why does SHE get to have a child, but not me? What's wrong with me? Why do you hate me?"

God didn't hate me at all.

Turns out, He knew better than I did all along. Had I gotten what I wanted any earlier, we never would have had the privilege of raising our precious little girl.

The excruciating seven-year wait resulted in the greatest joy we've ever experienced: being our daughter's parents.

We certainly weren't the first people who had to wait, and we won't be the last.

As Anna Bachinsky noted in an article that brought me tremendous comfort during the Great Big Wait:

> Jesus could have come and healed Lazarus when he was still alive. Instead, He waited to raise him from the dead when he was already in his grave.
>
> God could have made David become the king the day after he was anointed. Instead, He waited 15 years to rise to the throne. Many of those years spent fearing for his life, hiding out and running away from his own father-in-law.
>
> God could have given Abraham the son He promised him when he was a young man. Instead, He waited until he was 100 years old.
>
> God could have answered prayers and met the needs of these men quicker, but He didn't. He made them wait instead. And He often makes us do the same.[6]

DIVINE TIMING IS PERFECT TIMING

Although you may have had to endure tremendous suffering, waiting, heartbreak, or struggles along the way, know that there's perfect order to the process.

If you don't believe me, look at yourself in the mirror. Look at your body. Perfect order. Your heart beats an average of 115,200 times per day, without you doing a single damn thing.

You started off as microscopic egg and sperm, which miraculously joined together to kick-start a perfect process resulting in the creation of your heart, brain, legs, arms, fingers, toes, eyes—it's incredible!

Tiny microscopic cells also result in the creation of flowers, bugs, animals, vegetables, and trees. Chemicals combine perfectly to create oceans, mountains, valleys, and the air you breathe.

Order is all around you. Even the Earth rotates on its axis 24 hours a day, 365 days a year in perfect harmony, in divine timing, and subject to a divine order.

You're a divine creation and the beneficiary of a divine plan. While God's timing is typically *not* our timing, take comfort that there's a plan unfolding for you.

While that plan is unfolding, you'll be gifted lessons along the way that will prepare you to receive abundance in your life—happiness, health, wealth, success, joy, patience, gratitude, forgiveness, and more.

Embrace the lessons and enjoy the journey. Looking back on my journey to becoming a mother, had I simply trusted that God "had my back" all along, I would've experienced much less anxiety, worry, and sadness.

Divine timing is something I'm still learning to appreciate. It's certainly a process, although I'm becoming far more patient since witnessing amazing timing in action.

That said, your time is *now*. Not later. Not when the children are older, or when you have more free time or money or whatever. This is *your* time to start allowing your light to shine bright.

It's no coincidence that you picked up this book and are reading it right now. You're an Unstoppable Influencer, and it's time for you to begin your journey.

You may be just starting out trying to uncover your purpose and gifts. Throughout this book, I've equipped you with tools that will help you along the way.

Perhaps you already know your gift, but you've been playing small, as a hobbyist. You share your gifts only when you have "extra" time. If that's you, the time is *now* to level up your game and begin expanding your scope of influence.

Maybe you're already sharing your gifts, like Cristy, but aren't making the money you deserve and therefore aren't reaching the number of people you could. Your time is *now*—you've got to play a bigger game and unleash your influence in the world. Keep reading, and I'll show you how!

Again, it doesn't matter where you fall on the spectrum of Unstoppable Influence—beginner or more seasoned—the time is *now* to move to the next level.

I always share a great quote from Mary Morrissey at the beginning of my web classes: "Inspiration, without action, is merely entertainment."

While I certainly hope that I've entertained and inspired you so far, what I want most is for you to take *action*.

Don't worry, I'm not going to leave you hanging though as you're setting out on your journey. Turn the page and you'll discover the roadmap to Unstoppable Influence.

LET'S REVIEW

✤ Divine timing is perfect timing.

✤ There are no coincidences—perfect order is all around you.

✤ God has your back, no matter what.

✤ Take comfort in knowing that although divine timing is typically not your timing, an amazing plan is unfolding that's even bigger and better than you could ever imagine.

✤ Embrace the lessons gifted to you along your journey.

✤ Now is the time for you to begin your journey to becoming an Unstoppable Influencer.

✤ You must take action and unleash your influence in the world. Move from inspiration to action and don't look back.

TAKE ACTION NOW

1. Reflect on a time where you had to wait for something you wanted. What lessons did you learn while waiting? Were the rewards better than you expected?

2. Is there something you're waiting for currently? Pray or meditate on some activities that will prepare you to receive what you're waiting for.

3. Complete the 30-Day Action Plan in the *Companion Workbook* (UnstoppableInfluence.com/gift). How you will take action on what you've learned in this book? Compile all the steps you will take into the master list, then prioritize, assign dates, and put them on your calendar!

PART II

TRANSFORM LIVES:
YOUR ROADMAP TO
UNSTOPPABLE INFLUENCE

*If you want to achieve success, all you need to do
is find a way to model those who have already
succeeded.*

~ Tony Robbins

The lawyer in me always has to put order to a process. When I started coaching entrepreneurs back in 2010, I quickly realized that I led people through the exact same steps each time.

In an effort to save time for both me and my clients, I decided to document my process, and named it the Savvy Business Blueprint. This became the foundation of my signature program, *Branded: 100% Authentic.*

Likewise, after experiencing my own journey toward Unstoppable Influence, and in working with other Influencers on their journeys, I noticed a similar order. In the following chapters, I'll share it with you so you'll have your own track to run on. Sound good?

The roadmap to Unstoppable Influence has five main steps. Each step will encourage you to level up, face your fears, and unleash your influence in the world in a way that only you can.

Step 1: Find your voice and message.

Step 2: Determine who you'll serve.

Step 3: Identify how you'll serve your audience.

Step 4: Monetize your message.

Step 5: Unleash your influence and amplify your message.

CHAPTER 13

FIND YOUR VOICE AND MESSAGE

You can't find your voice if you don't use it.

~ Austin Kleon

Looking back on my journey to becoming an Unstoppable Influencer, surprisingly the hardest part *wasn't* losing 55 pounds or losing my business. For me, the most difficult part was finding my voice and message.

Early in my journey, my voice was chameleon-like, changing with my surroundings. I later discovered that this constant change was due to something I never knew I had.

AN APPROVAL ADDICTION

"Hi, I'm Natasha Hazlett, and I'm a recovering approval addict."

From a young age, I had an insatiable desire for approval from *everyone*: my mom, dad, friends, and teachers. This addiction wasn't all bad, though, because it fueled me to continually strive to improve in all areas of my life.

However, the dark side of this addiction appeared when I didn't get the approval I sought. I wasn't just sad or disappointed—I was devastated. The devastation further fueled my pre-existing feelings of never being good enough, sending me into a spiral of shame and, ultimately, full-fledged depression.

My Ego, always on a mission to "protect" me, would jump in and encourage me to change my voice to fit in and please others in the hopes of avoiding the pain of feeling not good enough.

MOVING ON

It wasn't until Rich and I finally packed up and moved 2,000 miles away from everything we knew that I was able to find my true voice.

You may not need such a radical shift, but I did. I needed the massively life-altering event of leaving my southern roots for Idaho to give myself permission to start exploring who I *really* was.

I was born in the small town of Greenwood, Mississippi, and grew up in Memphis, Tennessee. I adore the South. Where everything's just a little more formal and polite, people are oozing with kindness, and you just plain don't mess with tradition.

Tradition's a big thing down south, and so is society. When you're a part of the southern social scene, there are certain things you *can* and *cannot* do—especially if you're a lady. You must live in the right neighborhoods, belong to the right country club, attend the right schools, and belong to the right social clubs.

I was blessed that my family had the means for us to do all the "right" things. So it seemed like my life was pretty well set. My job? Don't screw up.

Knowing that finding my true voice would likely screw things up back home, I felt that I had no choice but to move.

The truth is, had I not left Memphis, I never would have had the courage to quit my attorney gig, which means you wouldn't be reading this book right now.

HAVE FAITH, DO IT SCARED

I know you're probably shuddering at the thought of picking up and moving across the country. But sometimes, if the situation calls for it, you just have to take a leap of faith.

If there's one recurring lesson I've learned over the years, it's this: Life is absolutely *yummy* when you choose to dance outside your comfort zone. All you need is faith and a willingness to do things while you're scared.

You won't always have the answers. But guess what? You don't *need* all the answers. Your desire to know everything before taking a step has caused your feet to be cemented inside your comfort zone, and that's dimming your light.

The great news is, though, that you have the power to change this at any time. One decision is all it takes—the decision to *live* outside of that zone.

You can put your trust in God because He won't lead you to a place then abandon you. Ever. You'll be equipped with everything you need for the journey. You show faith in Him, and He'll give you the runway you need to take off and soar.

Say *yes* when the opportunity calls.

Dr. Martin Luther King, Jr. once said, "Take the first step in faith. You don't have to see the whole staircase, just take the first step."

That's what I did. I just took the first step. I moved to Boise, Idaho, with my husband and we started a beautiful new life together.

THE DIRTY TRUTH ABOUT AUTHENTICITY

When I first started blogging, I began the process of finding my voice.

I say the "process" because it's exactly that. Seasons will come and go, as your voice matures and as you get closer to finding your true message.

You'll try many different voices until your Truth surfaces. That's okay!

You've likely noticed the trendy message over the years to "be your authentic self" or "just be you."

I followed that trend and even created a program called *Branded: 100% Authentic.* Ironically, though, as I was encouraging others to just be themselves, I myself wasn't operating in 100% authenticity.

Say what?

It wasn't intentional, of course. I truly believed I *was* being authentic, but I wasn't. I was depressed and uninspired for nearly three years, yet I never once shared that fact while I was busy preaching authenticity.

Who I thought I was wasn't in fact my reality. The stories I told myself were true turned out to be total BS. They were concocted by my Ego in a lame attempt to protect me from feeling inadequate.

It wasn't until I was able to identify those stories, peel back the layers, and do some deep work that I uncovered my *authentic* Truth.

BE BRAVE! PEEL BACK THE LAYERS

The first step in finding your *true* voice and message is committing to doing the work necessary to peel back the layers of your conscious mind to get to the goodies buried at your subconscious and soul level. This process may very well be outside your comfort zone. Do it anyway.

It is critical that you separate your Truth from fiction if you want to find your voice and message. That means you will have to do a little soul searching and be willing to call BS on stories that no longer serve you.

Who is making up these stories?

Your Ego, of course!

She's one helluva storyteller, let me tell you! As soon as you have a less-than-desirable experience, your Ego concocts a whole story around it. Then replays it like a movie anytime a similar event (or the possibility of a similar event) presents itself, all in the name of *protecting* you from a potentially undesirable consequence.

Likewise, if you have a desirable experience, your Ego creates a story around that and will play it again, in the name of helping you achieve the perceived benefit.

Most of the time, these stories—good or bad—are just BS.

Let me give you an example.

My grandmother, Teta, was the most amazing cook. Whenever I would go to Teta and Deeda's house, she showered us with love and affection, cooked delicious meals for all the grandkids, and treated us like the most important people in the world. Whenever we were sad, she'd cheer us up with a yummy treat. As a result, my Ego concocted a story about food that it replayed time and time again for over 30 years.

It went something like this: Food is good. When you love someone, you should cook food. When you're sad, food makes you feel better. Food is love. Food is comfort. When you feel bad, eat and you'll feel better.

As you read that, you're probably thinking, *That's ridiculous, Natasha. Food doesn't equal love. Especially if you're piling on the weight and hating yourself for it.*

I agree. But for years, my Ego replayed this story in my head, and I gained 60 pounds because of it.

The bottom line is, most of the time the stories in your head aren't true. If you look at them and ask, "Is that 100% true? Would others say this is 100% true?" Chances are, you'll realize that you're dealing with complete BS and can toss that story and write a new one.

You may be thinking, *Natasha, this sounds like lots of work that will come with an enormous therapy bill...*

Good news, you do not have to spend loads of money on therapists to uncover and rewrite these stories.

There are some amazing shortcuts to doing this kind of deep work. One of my favorite subconscious mind hacks is listening to pretty much anything by Joseph Clough.

Joseph is the certified hypnotherapist and neuro-linguistic programming magician I told you about earlier. His methods can quickly help you peel back the layers and tap into the power of your subconscious mind. It's like being able to peel an onion *without* the tears!

Pretty cool, right?

TEST OUT YOUR VOICE

The next step to finding your true voice is to *test* it out.

In my first attempt as a blogger, my voice was a tell-it-like-it-is style, and my message was about the incredible benefits of building a home business.

After I lost my business, I took a sabbatical of sorts. When I returned, my voice was the same, but the message had changed. This time, my message was the importance of building a personal brand online. I was focusing, at the time, on teaching people how to build their own brands and home businesses by blogging.

This message carried me through quitting my full-time attorney gig. However, I wanted my message to be more than simply teaching people about how to blog.

So I moved into teaching almost exclusively about branding—specifically how to define, build, and monetize a personal brand online. A couple of years later, I realized I really needed to stop being a me-too marketer, one who simply mimicked the voices and messages of successful people in my industry.

The challenge was that I didn't know what *my* voice and message really were. That's when I decided to do the unthinkable—record 100 videos. I committed to filming one video a day for 100 days. This idea was based on a training video I watched. By the 101st video, the program promised that you would find your voice.

So I did the videos. By the 101st video, I was most definitely comfortable in front of the camera. Unfortunately, this breakthrough was short-lived. The effects of my decision to sabotage myself with food caught up with me.

As I looked at the other women on video in my niche, then looked at myself on camera, my feelings of unworthiness began to take a toll.

I couldn't bear to watch myself on camera anymore. I hated seeing and hearing myself so much that I would tear up while watching my videos. I felt like no one would take me seriously. My videos weren't as professional, and I wasn't as pretty as my competitors.

Who would want to learn from me? I thought.

So I turned off the camera, ignored my blog, and the quest to find my voice and message came to an abrupt halt.

The fact that I was actively coaching my clients to step out of their comfort zones, quit comparing themselves to others, and just be authentic also took a toll on me because I felt like a fraud. I was doing everything I told my clients *not* to do. This made me retreat even further into my spiral of shame and doubt.

It wasn't until I decided to ditch the fat for good that I started progressing quickly toward my true voice and message. I knew the moment that I started my reinvention, I'd soon find my true self.

Instead of trying to be or act like someone else, I decided to listen to my inner voice and let the Spirit guide my message.

I also decided to go "public" on my personal Facebook page, and start doing regular Facebook Lives because I knew these raw, unedited videos would become an instrumental tool in my process of self-discovery.

I was right.

As a result of my decision to go public in a raw and vulnerable way, I was able to find my voice and my message. I realized just how out of alignment I had been. Operating out of alignment for so long had caused me to veer down the wrong path. Just like a car whose tires are out of alignment—it's hard to stay on the path when your car is getting pulled in the wrong direction.

For instance, my friends and family know that I have a tendency to swear from time to time.

Is it lady-like? Nope. So when I was out and about with anyone other than close friends and family, I kept things squeaky clean.

One day, I decided to take my swearing out from behind closed doors, and spice up a few of my Facebook Lives. Do you know what? It felt good.

I'm not one to drop swear words gratuitously, but sometimes the situation just calls for an f-bomb, and giving myself permission to deploy them as needed felt good because I finally started feeling more like me.

That said, I have a confession to make. As I started writing this book, I wasn't planning on swearing in it. Especially knowing that some family and friends may disapprove. Ultimately, I decided, in the words of Sir Richard Branson, "Screw it. Just do it."

Believe it or not, that still wasn't the biggest revelation about my voice and message.

The biggest "Oh shit" moment was when I realized, upon much meditation and prayer, that my message had a definite spiritual angle. So not only would I be swearing, I would also refer to the Big G quite frequently. Let's see how many people I can offend simultaneously—why the hell not?

I *finally* found the flow of my authentic message, and I know there are plenty of people who will resonate with my message and my voice.

The way I see it, I don't even *want* to please everyone. I don't need for everyone to love me (or approve of me). What a grand turnaround for the recovering approval addict, wouldn't you say?

Hopefully, by me sharing my journey, you'll realize that it's okay to be you, without compromising. Always remember that you could be the ripest, juiciest peach in the world, and there will *still* be people who don't like peaches. Just do you, and don't apologize for it.

AN UNLIKELY MESSAGE

Another fascinating angle to my message is that it's one of personal development and motivation. You have to understand how truly ironic this is for me.

When Rich and I first started dating, he told me about this guy named Tony Robbins, who he had been listening to since the age of 19.

I turned to him and said, in all seriousness, "What has personal development *done* for you?"

Since I'd been an overachiever for years due to my approval addiction, I never needed anyone to motivate me to do anything.

If I wanted something, I just went out and got shit done. I never understood why people needed to be motivated by something external, or to be taught how to set goals and believe in themselves. These skills came naturally to me.

So for years, while Rich listened to hundreds of books on Audible, I watched *The Bachelor* on TV. I never understood the true value of personal development until I hit rock bottom.

When I hit the bottom, I realized I'd been operating on autopilot, guided by my Ego. When the wheels came off and life didn't go the way I wanted, I didn't know how to handle it.

I discovered very quickly that I needed massive personal and spiritual growth if I was going to reach the number of people I was intended to serve. As I started investing in my own personal growth, I couldn't help but share my "a-ha" moments with others. I noticed that my friends and clients loved my messages, so I started talking more and more about personal growth.

It was around this same time that I had a massive epiphany: The one thing that determined the success or failure of a client's business was their mindset.

For years, I watched uber talented individuals walk away from their businesses, and it saddened me. It had nothing to do with the market or their talents or their marketing—it had everything to do with mindset.

I watched others who didn't have a lot of natural talent build businesses that made good money, because they had a "never quit" attitude and a commitment to personal growth.

On the other hand, we built marketing machine Ferraris for clients, handed them the keys, and put them in the driver's seat, yet they refused to put the car in gear and go. Why?

Mindset.

Because an Unstoppable mindset is one of the most important tools needed to be an Unstoppable Influencer, I knew that I would have to be the one to teach others how to make this mindset shift.

This was irony at the highest level. The girl who had actively avoided personal development was called to train others on that very same topic.

I could have avoided this part of my message if I wanted to. I could have said, "God, not me—I'm unprepared."

But if there's one thing I know, it's this: God equips those He calls. While you may not feel like the perfect person for the job you're called to do, have faith that you will be given every opportunity for growth, along with every necessary tool and resource. You must simply move forward in faith. Do things while you're scared. Then watch as miracles unfold around you, as you operate in alignment with your message and Truth.

After decades of struggle and feeling lost, I can now officially say that I'm operating in alignment with my Truth. It feels incredible. Creativity and joy flows effortlessly. I no longer waste my time obsessing over how others do or say things; I simply rely on my inner voice and operate in-Spirit. When I do, I know I'm sharing the message I came here to share, and it feels amazing.

It wasn't the prettiest, quickest, or easiest process to go through, but it yielded the perfect result.

I want you to experience a similar breakthrough.

So to wrap up, how do you know when you have found your true voice and message?

You know you're in the Truth Zone when…

- ❖ Your voice and message flow effortlessly.
- ❖ Each message you deliver feels good and not forced, even if it scares you.
- ❖ Others confirm that what you said was exactly what they needed to hear.
- ❖ It just feels right.

One final important thing that you must know about your voice and message is this—life is a collection of seasons, and there may come a time when you're called to shift your voice or message. Remain open, and welcome the change when and if it comes.

For now, I'm loving being in a place where I'm perfectly imperfect and sharing my authentic message with the world. I can't wait for you to experience the same clarity—I'm confident that you will.

LET'S REVIEW

- ❖ You may have to make some big changes to live in alignment with your voice and message.
- ❖ Life is yummy when you choose to dance outside your comfort zone.
- ❖ Have faith. Do things even while you're scared.

- Don't try to mold your voice or message to appeal to everyone. Be YOU, and don't you dare apologize.
- God equips those He calls. You may not feel like the perfect person for the message you're called to deliver, but have faith that you'll be given every opportunity, tool, and resource you need.
- You're in the Truth Zone when your voice and message flow effortlessly, even if it scares you.

TAKE ACTION NOW

1. Test out your voice by doing videos or Facebook Lives. For best results, record 101 of them. I double dog dare you! You do not need to map out the video topics, unless you feel more comfortable doing so. I took ordinary events and turned them into video topics. For example, a conversation with a client that sparked a good lesson. Or if I heard a great podcast or read something powerful in a book, I would share it on my next video.

2. Next time you're inclined to apologize for being *you*—don't. Saying "I'm sorry" when speaking your Truth diminishes its impact. You must never apologize for your Truth. Ever.

3. Make a list of 10 experiences you can have in the next 90 days that will make you a little uncomfortable. Do 3 of them in the next 30 days and post your progress in our Unstoppable Influence group at UnstoppableInfluence.com/group.

CHAPTER 14

PERFECTLY IMPERFECT

*Always be a first-rate version of yourself,
instead of a second-rate version of
somebody else.*

~ Judy Garland

One of the bigger challenges I faced over the past decade in
the "expert" industry was feeling like I was never quite "good
enough" yet. There was something else to read, a training
video to watch, or a conference to attend. Surely after I had
"enough" training, I'd be capable of stepping onto the stage
and sharing my message.

Yet no matter how many trainings or conferences I attended, I
never felt ready to launch my message in a big way. Why was
that?

Well, if it wasn't because of a lack of knowledge, then it was
because I wasn't "pretty" enough, lacked the money necessary
to purchase the high-quality production materials others had,
or someone else was launching their next big program at the
same time. It was *always* something.

At one point, the momentum we had in our business came to
a screeching halt. Then one day, one of my mentors, Russell

Brunson, said something that completely revolutionized the way I looked at myself in relation to my niche.

He said, "There's *never* gonna be a day that someone will tap you on the shoulder and say, 'You're ready. Here's your badge. You're an expert now!' "

Never.

No one's coming over with a crown, a trophy, or a sash, and no one's going to give you a damn permission slip to share your message.

You must stick your flag in the ground and say, "Here I am, and I'm ready to serve you!" Otherwise you'll be waiting around for something that will never happen, while depriving the world of your gift.

You're never going to be perfect. Never. That's not how it works.

You're perfectly imperfect, right now. One year from now, you'll still be perfectly imperfect. And 10 years from now? 20 years? 30 years? You guessed it—perfectly imperfect.

The ironic part is that it's your *imperfections* that make you *perfectly* qualified to share your message.

Hear me out. You wouldn't be the fab person you are today if you didn't experience life the way you've experienced it, warts and all.

The good and bad experiences built your character, your compassion, your empathy, your forgiveness, your patience, and pretty much every other good virtue.

In fact, it's the vulnerable backstories that cause me to build a strong bond with people and businesses. Take Marcus Lemonis, the ultrasuccessful businessman and star of CNBC's *The Profit*.

At a conference I attended, Marcus shocked the audience, who was expecting a business presentation, by opening up and sharing a very vulnerable part of his background. As I recount his story, think about how this affects the way you feel about him the next time you see him on TV or walk into one of his businesses.

******

Marcus was born in Beirut, Lebanon. He was abandoned as a child and lived in an orphanage. He was then adopted by an American family and moved to the United States. He was later molested as a child by a member of his extended family and even attempted suicide. Likely as a result of the trauma he suffered as a child, he became extremely overweight. He was bullied as a child, and ended up with an eating disorder.[7]

One day, Marcus awoke from the fog of his youth and went through a series of reinventions until he found himself and his purpose—he was a connector of people. Years later, he was mentored by Lee Iacocca, the former CEO of Chrysler. Iacocca suggested that Marcus enter the camping and RV business.

Marcus did just that, and he is now the CEO of Camping World and Good Sam, the #1 source for RVs and camping accessories in America. Currently, he is worth an estimated $1 billion, has a reality show on CNBC, and has invested nearly

$40 million of his own money to help struggling small-business owners turn their businesses around.[8]

Even better, Marcus started speaking to audiences around the country and opening up about his past. Marcus's story of his "awakening" (although he never called it that) had the effect of awakening me. I, in turn, have shared my story, which has awakened others. It's truly the epitome of the Ripple Effect.

******

Imagine throwing one small pebble into a pond. What happens? You see the big ripples created as a result. It's pretty impressive, actually. That little pebble has the ability to create a ripple 100 times bigger than itself.

One person—you—can be that little pebble. By stepping outside your comfort zone and sharing your message even just *once*, you can grow your sphere of influence by 100 times. Imagine what would happen if you shared that message 5 times…10 times…100 times or more. You can impact the world in a big, beautiful, and meaningful way even though you aren't Tony Robbins or Oprah Winfrey.

By now, you know that you're here *on* purpose and *for* a purpose. You're also here to learn, grow, and give to others, for the highest and best good of all. That means that throughout your life, you'll be given lessons to help you grow. As you grow, you can then help others along the way. This is why striving for perfection before sharing your message is pointless. Share your message while you're on your journey, don't wait to get to some perfect state before helping others.

The lessons help you grow, and they also give you a unique perspective that enables you to connect with other people.

For example, if one of the lessons you need to learn is patience, how could you ever learn how to be patient if you aren't given opportunities to practice it?

In fact, my client Angela knows she's intended to learn the lesson of patience because of a certain opportunity that has repeatedly shown up in her life: obnoxious neighbors.

No joke! Throughout her life, Angela has been plagued by one bad neighbor after another. Ones that peer into her windows, others whose dogs repeatedly poop in her yard, and some whose children continuously bounce their basketball on her car!

Honestly, if I were in Angela's position, I would have absolutely lost my shit by now. But not Angela. She knows that life gives you lessons to help you grow, and her string of annoying neighbors is God's way of giving her the opportunity to demonstrate and practice the virtue of patience.

You are perfectly imperfect just the way you are. It's through struggles and challenges that you'll not only grow, but you'll also become more relatable to those who follow your lead.

If you were perfect, not many people would want to follow you, because you'd be a reminder of their own inadequacies. It's by being your vulnerable and authentic self that you can connect on a deeper level with your audience. It's scary at first to be vulnerable, but know that so much yummy goodness will come of it. I've learned that lesson myself.

VULNERABILITY IN ACTION

The day I hired Cristy, I also began writing the talk I would give at my upcoming Branded Summit. I titled it Reinvention.

I wrote feverishly on that flight back to Boise, 15 pages to be exact. In that talk, I confessed to our very best clients that their "fearless" mentor hated herself. That she'd considered suicide. That she had struggled with disordered eating, and felt worthless, unlovable, and like a complete failure.

Not exactly the sexiest marketing message ever delivered, but the words just poured onto the page.

I took my pain to another level. The next day, as I drove to Cristy's office, I shot a video. When I rewatched the video months later, I was mortified. I looked like a glorified train wreck; it had captured all my raw emotion in that moment.

In my heart, I knew I needed to share my talk *and* the video, but my Ego said:

> You're a fool for doing this, Natasha. You'll lose *all* credibility with your clients. No one wants to learn from a hot mess. Who cares if you lost the weight? This is just poor positioning. Don't do it!

Luckily, I recognized this as Ego nonsense, and knew that I had to share my raw story, because it could change at least one person's life. That was reason enough for me.

I practiced my talk over and over again in the mirror. I was ready, or so I thought. Right before I walked on stage, I felt sick to my stomach. After collecting myself, I gave the talk and played the video.

As the lights came back on, there wasn't a dry eye in the room. One by one, my clients came up to hug me and tell me their stories. Many people's lives changed that day. My talk was a pivotal moment in their lives, just as Marcus's talk had been pivotal in mine.

Had I not gone through the depression, infertility, obesity, and everything else, I would not have been able to help the people I helped that day, or the ones who subsequently heard my story and transformed their own lives.

Perfection was never required. In fact, it was the imperfection that allowed me to serve others best.

You're perfectly imperfect. Embrace it, and share your message with the world *now*. The world is waiting for you, so don't keep them waiting any longer.

LET'S REVIEW

- ❖ There will never be a day when you feel completely ready to launch yourself out there as an Influencer. You must jump before you feel ready.
- ❖ No one will give you a crown, sash, or certificate entitling you to be an Unstoppable Influencer. Put your flag in the ground and *own* it.

- ❖ You're perfectly imperfect. Your imperfections are what make you perfect.

- ❖ Be the pebble in the pond. Take the action necessary to create the Ripple Effect in the world. You can make an impact 100 times greater just by one small action.

- ❖ You're here to learn, grow, and give to others, for the highest and best good of all. As you grow, you have the ability to help others along the way.

- ❖ You are who you are today because of the bad (and good) experiences. Embrace it, own it, and use it to positively impact the world.

TAKE ACTION NOW

1. Write your story, warts and all.

2. How can your story help others? What lessons can someone take from hearing your story?

3. Embrace your perfectly imperfect self and record a Facebook Live video. Tell the world who you are and what you do. Add the hashtag #UnstoppableInfluencer to the end, then share it in the Unstoppable Influence Community at: UnstoppableInfluence.com/group

4. Watch Brené Brown's TED Talk "The Power of Vulnerability."

CHAPTER 15

WHO WILL YOU SERVE?

The meaning of life is to find your gift.
The purpose of life is to give it away.

~ Picasso

Who are you intended to serve? That's the million-dollar question, isn't it? The good news is you can't really make a wrong choice, except perhaps refusing to make one at all.

When you see people on TV like Oprah, Dr. Oz, Tony Robbins, or other megastars, it can be intimidating, I know. You may feel as if you're not good enough. You may get overwhelmed trying to figure out how to even begin impacting an audience that large.

But you have two powerful concepts operating in your favor. First, there's the Ripple Effect. Even if you only impact one person's life, that person can then impact two people's lives, and then those people can do the same for other people. Just one action can cause a series of events that result in thousands, tens of thousands, or even millions of lives being transformed.

In fact, Rich and I were recently reminiscing about how we got to be where we are today. It all started with one of his college buddies, Steven Thompson. Steven joined a network marketing company and told Rich all about it. Together they dreamed of the fabulous wealth and impact they could make through their business. Rich joined that company, and he experienced success initially, but the company ultimately went out of business. Long story short, Rich decided to quit network marketing, but Steven didn't.

One day, a mutual friend asked Rich if he had heard how Steven was doing. Rich said he had not. The friend then handed him a copy of *Millionaire Magazine*. Sure enough, his friend Steven was on the cover.

From that day forward, Rich vowed to never quit pursuing success in his own business. Many years later, when I heard Steven's story, I was blown away. Once I saw the amazing impact Steven and others were making, I caught the entrepreneurial bug and never looked back.

Here's the cool part—when Steven Thompson was just getting started in his business, he simply reached out to Rich to share his opportunity. That's it.

This one conversation has resulted in our decade-long business of serving tens of thousands of people around the world, and this book, which I'm confident will ultimately impact millions of lives.

Everyone has to start somewhere. Lao Tzu was spot on: "The journey of a thousand miles begins with one step."

START WITH ONE STEP

When we met, Cristy was solely focused on serving people in Idaho, but when I experienced her gift for myself, I knew she had to share her message with a much larger audience.

As I sat in her office, we discussed the people she felt called to serve. Turns out, I wasn't even in her demographic! She felt called to help women who were in their 50s and 60s who felt frumpy, had neglected themselves for years while raising children, and were ready to take their lives back.

So that's who she focused on serving. As we worked on amplifying Cristy's message (more on this in Chapter 20), other people outside her intended group joined in. Once they had experienced Cristy's life changing message, they shared it with others—and the Code Red Revolution was born.

Cristy's ultimate desire is to revolutionize the food industry by putting warning labels on food with sugar and other toxins and disseminating accurate nutrition information. However, she had to start somewhere. So do you.

For me, identifying the people I'm intended to serve has been a journey best summed up as follows:

There's a season for everything.

I began my journey by serving individuals who wanted to quit their full-time jobs and start home-based businesses. My audience later narrowed to direct-sales professionals who wanted to build personal brands online.

A few years later, I focused on serving coaches and consultants looking to monetize their personal brands online. Today, I'm called to serve experts looking to boost their income and impact in the world without working longer hours.

It was a process. I had to start somewhere, just like you do. As I evolved as an individual and as an entrepreneur, so did my audience.

FEAR OF MAKING A MISTAKE

When it comes to figuring out who you're intended to serve, you first need to consult your Source by meditating or praying.

All too often, when it comes to business, you may toss God to the side, because you think, "Hey, I got this."

Your Ego makes you *think* you've got all the answers when you really don't. Years ago, I mentioned to a friend that I have the greatest business partner in the world. They said, "Oh, that's so sweet to say about Rich!"

I said, "Oh, him too. But I was actually referring to God."

I consult God frequently in my business. My thought is, why *not* go to the Source of infinite wisdom to ask for guidance? It sure takes the pressure off of me having to come up with the right answers.

It's a pretty simple thing to do. Just make time to meditate and ask, "Who am I intended to serve right now?" You'll get a response.

Once you get the response, you can do what I do—ask for confirmation or clues that you're on the right path.

Then watch as the clues begin to surface out of seemingly nowhere. It may be a book that you feel compelled to read, something you see on TV, or a message that comes through your Facebook feed. Often the subject will come up in conversation, or you may be introduced to a person who is totally your ideal client.

When it comes to picking the right audience, when you're truly tuning in to your Source, the answer you get will never be wrong. Here's why.

Even if you pick the "wrong" audience, there will be a lesson contained in that choice that will lead you to the "right" audience. It's a can't-lose proposition. Sometimes you need to serve one audience for a while because that experience will equip you to serve your next audience.

WHO NEEDS YOU? FINDING YOUR IDEAL CLIENT

"If you're marketing to everyone, you're marketing to no one." There's truth to this old saying.

Not *everyone* will be a perfect fit for you. There are people who you love working with, and there are those you don't enjoy working with. There are people who are willing and able to pay you for your products and services, and there are people who are unwilling or unable to pay you.

The people you enjoy working with but are unwilling or unable to pay you are what I like to refer to as the "brain pickers." They are the ones who will take you out to lunch to snag some free advice. They are NOT your ideal clients.

Then there are the individuals you don't really like working with, but who are willing and able to pay you. These are the nightmare clients or "soul suckers" who typically drain your energy and your joy. They are also NOT your ideal clients.

Finally, there are people who you love working with and are willing and able to pay you what you're worth. They are your ideal clients.

Most marketing experts use something called an *ideal customer avatar* to help a business owner identify the individuals who are the "right fit" for their business. They encourage consideration of details such as gender, age range, income level, marital status, and geographic area.

The challenge I always faced with this exercise is that I never felt connected to what I wrote. This sort of sterile assessment of who I would serve never inspired me, and although I diligently completed the exercise, it never worked for me.

One day, I decided to really hone in on who I wanted to serve, so I created a whole story about her, complete with a name, the names and personalities of her family members, and other details of her life. I even googled to find a picture of what I thought she might look like.

Within weeks, my calendar was filled with people who looked just like Betty Adams, my perfect client. When we hosted our first live workshop, over 80% of the audience was just like Betty.

Rumor has it that I'm not the only one who has used this method. After writing my own Perfect Client story, I learned about a successful businessman who pitched his product to a big box store. At the end of his sales pitch, the buyers in the boardroom looked around at each other and said, "I'm not sure Julie would really like this product."

Being the exceptional salesperson he was, the fella told the buyers he'd like to schedule a meeting with Julie. They laughed and said it might be a little hard to do that, then pointed to a picture of a woman on the wall. Turns out, Julie was the company's perfect customer.

After hearing this story, and based upon my own experience, I encouraged my clients to do the same thing—write their Perfect Client story.

My sister-in-law, Kendra, was about to launch her first book, *Common Sense and an Uncommon God: A Patriotic Devotional.* Since she was in my *Branded: 100% Authentic* program at the time, she used my Perfect Client template to create Patriotic Patty, her ideal reader. She used Patriotic Patty to target her marketing, and her book was downloaded from Amazon 3,500 times within the first 36 hours of her launch.

Not long after Kendra's phenomenal success, another one of my students, James, reported that two days after completing the Perfect Client template, he got a call from a prospect who sounded just like he'd imagined and was only two years older. Not only that, the prospect became James's next client.

I'm no Law of Attraction guru, but I can't discount the fact that this law appears to be at work when people use the Perfect Client template.

As my gift to you, you can download the exact template that Kendra, James, and thousands of others have used to attract the perfect client or customer to your business at NatashaHazlett.com/template

LET'S REVIEW

❖ Even if you positively influence just one person's life, the Ripple Effect will cause your impact to grow exponentially with no additional effort on your part.

❖ Everyone has to start somewhere. The audience you serve initially may not be the audience you serve forever.

❖ Even if you pick the "wrong" audience at first, the experience will equip you to serve your next audience.

❖ Remember that your Creator is an *awesome* business partner. Connect frequently.

❖ When you're determining your audience, write a story about your perfect client or customer, and let the Law of Attraction go to work for you.

TAKE ACTION NOW

1. Meditate or pray about the group you'll serve first. Who do you enjoy working with? Who can benefit the most from your gifts?

2. Write your Perfect Client story using the Perfect Client template at NatashaHazlett.com/template.

3. Once you write your story, find a picture of your perfect client and add it in!

CHAPTER 16

IT'S NOT ABOUT YOU!

Change your thoughts and you
change your world.

~ Norman Vincent Peale

So many times when you study the concept of influence in marketing, business, or leadership, it's all about the Influencer. That's BS, because it really isn't all about you!

(Cue the record screech.)

Now hear me out on this one. A positive influence in the purest sense of the word is a gift. It's a gift you give to someone whose life will change because of you.

I remember sitting at a business mastermind lunch one day with Anne. We'd met in passing the week earlier and had instantly clicked as friends.

Anne clearly was a gifted coach. When the time came for her to be in the mastermind "hot seat," she told us that she truly wanted to take her business online and help other people, but...

She'd had a costly string of bad luck with web designers and marketers promising her the world and then not delivering the goods. None of the people she'd hired in the past could ever bring her vision to light. Plus, she claimed that she sucked at technology. So she'd pretty much given up on the concept of turning her hobby into a real business that would impact the world. She wanted our opinion on this dilemma.

Being the no-BS coach that I am, I asked Anne for permission to be ultra honest with her, out of love. She said, "Of course, bring it on!"

So I did.

"Anne, you're being selfish."

(Cue heads snapping around to stare at me in disbelief.)

Anne's eyes widened, but thankfully, instead of bitch-slapping me, she allowed me to continue.

I said, "You're selfish because you're making this all about you. There are people you don't even *know* yet who are counting on you to succeed and put yourself out there. If you aren't out there, they may *never* learn the truth about how abundance can transform their lives.

"God gifted you with the knowledge of how to live an abundant life. Not only is it a good idea for you to get your message out there, you have a *duty* to do so. You have a *duty* to massively succeed in your business. You can't be given an incredible gift and then play small. It's selfish!"

Taking a deep breath, she said, "You're right."

(Cue exhales from the group.)

That's the cold, hard truth. When you're blessed with a gift—a bright light that can transform people's lives—it's your *obligation* to share it with the world. You were blessed with a gift so you would *share* it, not keep it to yourself!

I had learned that lesson years earlier. I would oftentimes think about what would've happened had I not returned to our business. Whose lives would not have been touched?

- Alice, the software engineer who desperately wanted to stay home with her children. I helped Alice launch a business that was her family's saving grace when she was unexpectedly laid off from her job.

- Heather, the direct-sales professional, whose team was the only one benefiting from her powerful message. Had Heather not worked with me, she may never have launched her own business enabling her to easily touch tens of thousands more lives.

- Cristy would've continued to toil away for $30,000 *a year* for the next 15 years, thereby depriving the world of her revolutionary way to lose weight and stay healthy. Now she earns an average of over $40,000 *per month* in her business, and her message is reaching thousands of people daily.

Not to mention the tens of thousands of lives touched by our trainings and events over the years. I get choked up just thinking of what my life and the lives of others would've looked like if I hadn't shown up in our business and continued to master my message and gifts.

This is why I say being an Unstoppable Influencer isn't about you; it's about helping others by sharing your gifts.

Can you imagine Santa Claus flying around on Christmas Eve with all the toys in his sleigh, never once stopping on a rooftop or sliding down the chimney to share those gifts? Me neither. Don't be a Grinch—share your gifts. Just like Santa, it's your job!

Anne isn't a Grinch, and neither are you. The reason ultra gifted folks end up sidelined has *nothing* to do with being selfish. It has everything to do with that pesky Ego character.

Your Ego comes into the picture and tells you nonsense like:

> "Suzy is WAY better at this, plus she's been doing it longer."
>
> "There are too many coaches/speakers in the world, so you'll just get lost in the crowd."
>
> "Mark is fit, good-looking, and has tons of money. You're fat and broke. You don't stand a chance. Why would anyone want to work with you?"

Here's what I discovered, though. People like you who have Unstoppable Influencer DNA are givers. You're naturally generous. So the moment you realize that keeping your gifts is selfish, you're far more inclined to put all the emotional baggage aside for a hot minute to help others.

The more people you help, the more confidence you'll build. The more confidence you gain, the more willing you'll be to work on releasing the toxic emotions you've been carrying around.

That was certainly my experience, and the experience of those I've coached over the years. When it's not about *you*, but instead about others in need, it becomes far easier to share your light.

There will come a time when you'll want (and need) to address the BS that's been holding you back. But that should never keep you from sharing your light in the meantime. There's always going to be someone better, smarter, skinnier, or richer than you. Share your light anyway.

There are people far better than I am at applying spiritual principles to business and marketing. However, that's no longer stopping me, because I'm Unstoppable.

Some people just need to hear it from me—the way I say it, swear words and all. Likewise, there are people who need *your* gift, in the way *you* deliver it. So don't waste precious time comparing yourself to others.

The only person you need to compare yourself to is YOU. Today, are you a better YOU than you were yesterday? If not— you've got work to do, so get to it!

LET'S REVIEW

- ✤ Being an Influencer is not about you. Don't be a Grinch; share your gifts. (But if you're an entrepreneur, charge for them. See Chapter 18 if this concept freaks you out.)
- ✤ The world is darker if you don't share your light.
- ✤ You have a duty to succeed. People you don't even know yet are depending on you to show up!

❖ At some point, you'll need to address the baggage that's been holding you back, but don't let it stop you from sharing your light in the meantime.

❖ There are people who need your gift, in the way that YOU deliver it. So don't waste precious time comparing yourself to others. The only person you need to compare yourself to is YOU. Are you a better YOU today than you were yesterday? If not, you have work to do.

TAKE ACTION NOW

1. Make a list of your gifts and then reflect on whether you're sharing them as much and as often as you should be. If not, commit to leveling up your game so you can make a greater impact.

2. Reflect on what beliefs or situations may be holding you back. What steps can you take to overcome these perceived challenges?

3. Take one personal growth action step each day to become a better you. Read for five minutes, listen to a podcast, watch a web class, attend a workshop, or step outside your comfort zone.

CHAPTER 17

HOW WILL YOU SERVE?

Today you are you. That's true-r than true.
There's no one alive, that's youer than you!

~ Dr. Seuss

When I first started my business, I hated having competitors. They intimidated the hell out of me. When I saw others with more resources who were better looking or had more experience, I felt deflated and out of my league.

But I had it all wrong—competition is actually a really *good* thing. It means there are people looking for what you're offering. When you're first to market, you're the guinea pig. You may strike gold, but it's more likely that you'll run out of money first, because it's easier to go into a proven market. If there are competitors making money, that means there are plenty of buyers out there, which is great news.

When I tell my clients that, they're shocked.

"You mean competition in my niche is *good*?" they ask. My response is always a resounding "Yes!"

Then comes the follow-up. "But Natasha, there are SO many Xs out there already. I'll be a tiny minnow in the ocean!"

Here's what I say:

> What if Oprah Winfrey had said, "There are already plenty of talk show hosts; there's no room for me!"
>
> Or if Johnny Carson had thought, "There are already plenty of comedians, so why bother?"
>
> What if Tony Robbins had decided, "There are already plenty of speakers. I couldn't possibly compete."

The reality is, there's only *one* you. There are people out there who need what *you* have to offer, in the way that *you* offer it. Don't let the compare-itis bug get you, like it got me for years.

My obsession with the more successful competitors in my industry nearly sidelined me for three years. (Newsflash: When you're on the sidelines, you aren't helping anyone.)

When I was getting ready to launch *Branded: 100% Authentic* for the first time, I had been working on it for months. Two weeks before the launch, I discovered that Sarah, another woman in my industry, was about to launch her own marketing course.

We were teaching completely different marketing strategies, but that didn't matter to me. All I cared about was that Sarah was skinnier and prettier than me. Plus, she had a bigger business budget, so she could afford professional video production quality and marketing materials. I was doing everything on my own, so I was resentful that my launch didn't look nearly as nice.

Sarah's launch started the week before mine. With each video she posted, my confidence shrunk. I cried to Rich daily about my misfortune. How could she launch right before I did? Why don't we have the money to hire all the professionals like she did?

Honestly, I was a total pain in the ass to be around. Looking back, I feel sorry for Rich. One day he'd had enough and said I wasn't allowed to look at another one of Sarah's videos ever again. I didn't, and life got better for both of us.

We launched Branded, and although it may not have generated millions of dollars, it profoundly transformed many lives. To me, that was worth way more.

Here's the thing—it's important to know your competition. The key is to not obsess like I did. Now I remind my clients to "Stay in your own damn lane!"

Otherwise your Ego will rear its ugly head and entice you to engage in the self-sabotaging practice of comparing yourself to everyone. That will send you into a downward spiral of self-doubt.

Here's the reality: You're awesome just the way you are. You're capable of serving your audience in the way they need to be served. Don't waste a moment worrying about what other people are doing—do your business, your way.

That said, remember that you need to know the competition in your industry, so you can learn how and where they're marketing, and develop your own UIP—Unique Influencer Proposition.

How do *you* do business in a way that's different from your competitors? If you don't do anything differently, you need to look at how you can distinguish yourself moving forward.

This is another one of those times when you need to reconnect with your Source. Let your Creator guide you about how you can do business differently. Once you receive the inspiration you need, it's time to put it into action.

HOW YOU CAN SERVE OTHERS (AND GET PAID)

I can't tell you how many times I've seen ultratalented people just sitting on the sidelines. They're giving away their expertise for free because they're afraid people won't find value in their offer, or worse, they think they're not good enough yet.

You're ready now. Even if you have to price yourself slightly lower for the first few sales just to boost your confidence. With my first coaching package, I sold five 1-hour sessions for $250. What a steal of a deal they got! Now I charge $750 per hour, but I had to start somewhere. And so do you.

If you're a consultant, coach, or other type of solo-practitioner, one-on-one services will help you get to know your perfect client, so you can create additional offerings to serve them in the future.

Starting out with *something*, even a one-on-one service, can be of tremendous benefit, as opposed to waiting to invent the best and most perfect thing on the planet.

Remember that it's not all about you.

It's about the people who will benefit from your products and services. When you come from a desire to serve others, it's a hell of a lot easier to get out of your own damn way.

If you're not sure which direction to go in serving your audience, meditate or pray first. A warning though—for this method to work, you must be *open* to receiving the information, and then *take action* in faith.

A perfect example of this concept is the book you're holding in your hands. I knew that the time had come for me to create a new program and spread a new message. Because I was so used to creating digital programs, I assumed that I would serve my audience with another home-study program.

That, admittedly, was my Ego talking. She was rationally leading me to what made the most sense based upon all the information and experience I had.

However, as the time for me to sit down and create the program grew closer, I discovered through prayer and meditation that a book was the best method to serve my audience initially.

That was a shocker! I'd never even written a book. My last attempt had ended a third of the way through. Besides, I didn't know how to write a book, much less publish one. Even worse, I didn't want to take the time to learn how.

But ever since I began my reinvention, I've been committed to remaining open to new experiences and dancing outside my comfort zone. So I accepted the challenge.

Within a week of my decision, I received a call from my friend Julie Eason, who had just launched her Non-Fiction Book Academy and asked if I would be interested in participating as a Beta tester—an unmistakable sign that I was on the right path.

I didn't know how to write a book, yet I was led to simply make the time to write—I started typing and just let the words flow.

And flow they did.

I just needed to be open and trust my Creator to lead me down the right path.

When it came to the editing and publishing of this book, I wasn't concerned either. I knew the right resources would be revealed at the right time.

The greatest lesson I've learned on my journey is that you're not expected to have all the answers. You don't *need* all the answers about how you'll serve.

This certainly bugs Lawyer Natasha, who likes to have all her ducks lined up in a perfect row, but God has proven Himself to me, time and time again.

My best advice?

Release your inner control freak.

When you're operating in alignment with God's plan, you can rely on Him 100% to equip you with the tools, resources, words, and support you need, when you need them.

Notice I said "when you need them," because that's *really* important. If God dumped everything out in advance, you'd be overwhelmed. He knows that. So take the journey one step at a time.

The next step for me was to create and launch our Unstoppable Influence Home-Study program. It didn't stop there, though. Rich and I are serving our audience through our annual Unstoppable Influence Summit, where we bring together the world's most brilliant minds to connect with our Unstoppable Influencer family in a jam-packed transformational event.

In the future, I am certain there will be additional ways for us to serve others, but my job is moving into action on the plans I know about, not worrying about what may happen in the future.

The same lessons I have learned apply to you and your mission. Have confidence and move forward in faith in order to serve your audience in the highest and best way possible. Make sure you've got your own Unique Influencer Proposition, and do not be afraid to charge what you're worth!

LET'S REVIEW

* There is only *one* you. There are people who need what you have to offer, the way that you offer it.
* Avoid the compare-itis bug, because it can infect you for years.
* It's important to know your competition, but don't obsess. Remember to stay in your own damn lane!

- ❖ Start out offering *something*, even a one-on-one service, instead of waiting to invent the best and most perfect thing on the planet.

- ❖ If you're sitting on the sidelines, you aren't helping anyone.

- ❖ It's not about you—it's about the people who will benefit from your products and services.

- ❖ You're not expected to have all the answers. In fact, you don't NEED to have all the answers about how you'll serve people. Just be open, connect to God, and let Him guide you.

TAKE ACTION NOW

1. How will you serve your audience?

2. Who else is serving your audience? How will your Unique Influencer Proposition encourage buyers to do business with *you*?

3. The next time you catch yourself comparing yourself to others, say this out loud: "I'm staying in my own damn lane. I'm me, and that's all I need to be!"

4. Charlie "Tremendous" Jones used to say, "Many times the greatest idea you get from a coach, consultant, or speaker is not something he or she says… it's something you think of as a result of what they say!" He was absolutely correct. When you hear an idea, your creativity kicks in, and you extrapolate the specific takeaway you were looking for. Write down 3–5 ideas you've had so far.

CHAPTER 18

LET'S TALK ABOUT MONEY, HONEY!

Money isn't the most important thing in life, but it's reasonably close to oxygen on the 'gotta have it' scale.

~ Zig Ziglar

Down south, most people would cringe at this chapter title. Talking about money is so "tacky" and taboo that we don't usually talk about it.

Screw that!

Money's neither a bad thing nor a good thing. It's just a *thing*.

Money does, however, allow you to buy the products and services you need. And it's okay to want things too. Money is not evil. It is the love of money that can cause problems.

When you have the tools and resources you need to unleash your influence in the world, that's a *good* thing! So let's dive in and talk about money, because it will fuel your influence.

Remember the important lessons I received through my 4:30 a.m. "download"? One of them was that money would be critical to reaching my desired level of influence.

Up until this point, money had never motivated me. Plenty of people in the personal development and business niche have compelling rags-to-riches stories—I'm not one of them.

I was raised in an affluent family, never really wanting for anything. I lived in a large, beautiful home, went to one of the best private schools, and spent many summers traveling abroad.

Fortunately, my parents were humble and levelheaded people, and this rubbed off on my brother, George, and me. We were always grateful for what we had, never demanded anything, and were taught early on the importance of giving generously to those less fortunate.

That said, since I had everything I wanted and needed, money never motivated me. While many of my colleagues were fueled by a desire to make six-, seven-, or eight-figure incomes, those goals never lit my fire, because I knew that no amount of money could bring me happiness. Stuff is just that—stuff.

So imagine my surprise when I discovered that I needed to focus on money to achieve my goals. What I'm about to say may piss some people off, but here it goes…

Yes, money can help you acquire the resources you need as an Unstoppable Influencer. What's *more* important though is the fact that money is a magnet. More specifically, it's a people magnet.

When you have a dream house and pictures from fabulous trips, people pay attention. Most people desire more money because they believe it will bring freedom and happiness. When people believe you can give them these things, they will follow you and listen to what you have to say. And then you have the opportunity to share your Truth and influence their lives in a positive way.

Once I understood that money could be a powerful tool used for *good* instead of the selfish pursuit of material things, I decided to make more money. I asked for it, and then began preparing for the "rain" so I could reap the bountiful harvest.

So for all of you "money isn't important to me" people out there, consider for a moment that money *might* be the tool you need to attract people so you can transform lives.

Remember money is neither good nor bad. It just is. It's what you do with the money that makes the difference.

That said, there's a Bible verse that I love and frequently quote: "From everyone who has been given much, much will be demanded; and from the one who has been entrusted with much, much more will be asked." Luke 12:48 (NIV)

You've been blessed with an incredible, powerful gift. When you share that message as it was intended, watch as abundance pours into your life.

Cristy is a perfect example of this concept in action. She shared her gift for 15 years and was transforming lives, but she wasn't serving the number of people she was capable of serving.

But remember: Everything happens in divine timing.

God perfectly orchestrated our paths crossing—for me when I needed her help to uncover my Truth from underneath the mounds of fat, and for Cristy when she needed help figuring out how to share her message in a bigger way.

So don't think you're behind. You aren't. You picked up this book at the *perfect* time.

When we met, Cristy was only serving 80 to 100 people annually and making an average of $30,000 per year, yet she was working around the clock. Hardly the level of income or influence she desired.

When we started working together, we mapped out how she could serve the largest number of people in the *best* way possible. This plan didn't happen overnight; the process evolved over a 12-month period.

During our first year working together, Cristy discovered tools to scale her business and new ways to serve her audience, even if they hadn't purchased one of her coveted custom nutrition programs. This was an important piece of the puzzle, because Cristy's message was far too powerful not to share on a large scale. Her Code Red Lifestyle is a powerful tool enabling people to awaken from the "food fog" that's been destroying their bodies for decades

Recently, Cristy launched three 45-day weight-loss challenges. The first challenge had 35 people, the next one grew to 218, and the latest exploded to over 1,247 participants. That's 1,500 lives that have been impacted by her message within 9 short months!

Her income reflects that impact. Cristy made an impressive $174,000 in a single month! That's quite the contrast to her former annual income of $30,000, don't you think?

Financial abundance is flowing into Cristy's life at a massive rate. However, she knows that to whom much is given, much is expected, so she's using her financial abundance to bless those less fortunate while also reinvesting in her business so that her circle of influence will continue to expand.

She's willing to do whatever it takes to save people's lives. In fact, I believe that because of Cristy, the food industry will transform much like the tobacco industry has over the years.

There are several important takeaways from this part of Cristy's story.

First, the notion that you must put in the hours for each dollar you earn is an antiquated one that has people chained to a desk and a clock. It's causing them to unnecessarily limit their scope of influence.

Instead, you should be compensated for the *value* you bring to the marketplace, not the number of hours you work.

If a brain surgeon was going to charge you $30,000 for a life-saving brain surgery, would you get pissed off if the surgery lasted only 30 minutes? Would you insist that the surgeon operate on your brain for 24 hours to "get your money's worth"? I hope not!

People will *gladly* pay for good results. Cristy offers her clients transformational results, and people are more than happy to pay $1500 or more to work with her for 30 days. That's triple what she was charging when we first started working together.

Plus, Cristy's personal deliverables have been drastically reduced. Clients love the level of service they receive from her, and now she has plenty of time to tend to her relationships and engage in self-care. It's a win-win.

YOU'RE WORTH IT!

The next lesson might make you uncomfortable, but we must address it. Let's talk about what you're worth. (Spoiler Alert: It's way more than you think!)

Most people who are blessed with a gift have a *really* hard time charging appropriately for it.

Some feel guilty charging for something gifted to them by God. Others have money issues such as "I'm not worth $x" or "I'm afraid people won't pay $x" or "So-and-so only charges $y, so I have to be cheaper." Cristy certainly wrestled with several of these issues herself.

The reality is that most money issues stem from BS stories you're telling yourself. The stories are simply *not* true. They're concocted by your Ego to protect you from what it perceives to be bad or dangerous.

For example, if your Ego has experienced the feeling of rejection (and we all have)—it equates rejection with "bad." Your Ego wants to avoid "bad" at all costs. So anytime there's a possibility of rejection, your Ego raises the red flag, sounds the alarm, and tries to steer you clear of *any* possible rejection.

The reality, though, is that rejection (while it may sting) is not a life or death situation—like say, for instance, a lion chasing you. Your Ego, however, doesn't know the difference between life or death situations and temporary disappointments. Just like a lion chasing you is bad, your Ego equates rejection to being chased by a lion—therefore, it's a situation to be avoided at all costs.

Essentially, your subconscious mind is overdramatizing the effect of something like rejection, and that's keeping you from getting paid what you're worth.

You *must* charge and receive what you're worth. Money may not buy you happiness, but it can certainly buy the things you need to grow your scope of influence. So if you need money to fulfill your purpose, you're gonna need to get comfortable ask ing for it. Why? You must do whatever it takes to spread your message as far and wide as possible.

If you're broke, it will be difficult to spread your message in a big way.

Remember God *wants* to give you the tools you need to succeed on your mission. He would never "call" you to do something and then not equip you to succeed. That's not how He works.

From a strategic business perspective, when I talk to my clients about monetizing their messages and how to price their products and services, I always start by asking this question:

What is the transformative value you bring to people's lives?

This is important, because there's a huge difference between *price* and *value*.

Price is the amount of money someone pays for your product or services. *Value* is the monetary equivalent of the transformation your client experiences. Let me give you an example.

The first program that Cristy enrolled in cost $10,000. As a result of following my advice, she tripled her income in 30 days and then hit 6 figures for the first time in her 15+ years in business. In her twelfth month on the program, she earned $32,000. Overall, Cristy generated more than $100,000 in additional revenue because of the $10,000 program she had participated in, *plus* she received the knowledge she needed to continue making awesome money in the future.

The *price* of the program Cristy completed was $10,000. Yet its *value* exceeded $100,000 because Cristy's revenue was just one indicator of the value she received. On top of the money she made, she also reduced her workload by two-thirds, was able to stop paying for office space, and spent an entire month snowboarding with her husband.

How do you put a value on time, freedom, and a closer relationship?

Not surprisingly, Cristy didn't bat an eye when it came time to renew her membership in our yearly coaching program. She immediately signed up for our highest-level program at the time, which cost $30,000.

Cristy shared with me that within three weeks, as a result of the strategies she learned while working with us, she had already made $40,000. Two months later, her *monthly* revenue hit $174,000! Not to mention the fact that she's now well on her way to being on the big stage and sharing her message with the world.

What do you think the value of our Platinum coaching program is to Cristy? Likely a million dollars or more, since that's what she'll make because of the knowledge she now has after investing in our coaching program.

Another example is Heather, the top direct-sales distributor who invested $10,000 to learn how to monetize her own unique message online, outside of her direct-sales company. She learned how to generate leads online and, as a result, grew a list of thousands of prospects for her business. No longer must Heather attend coffee or lunch meetings to build her business. This frees up even more time to spend with her family.

Heather also closed a $10,000 coaching client in her business and created digital training products that bring in the coveted SWISS dollars. She now also has a powerful personal brand that she loves and feels confident with.

What is the *value* of our coaching program to Heather? She would likely tell you it's at least 10 times what she actually paid for it.

The moral of these stories is this: When pricing your products and services, strongly consider the transformational value of what you bring to the marketplace, instead of just looking at what other businesses actually charge.

As people began to experience life-changing transformations as a result of Cristy's program, they willingly paid her $1,000 for a customized nutrition program. Her competitors charge a fraction of this price, yet this has no effect on all the people lining up to pay Cristy what she's worth—even if it requires taking out a loan.

Do you get great results for your clients and customers? If so, charge what you're worth. Remember that you owe it to yourself, and to everyone who is counting on you to succeed.

LET'S REVIEW

- ❖ Money is neither good nor bad. It just is. It's what you do with money that makes the difference.
- ❖ Most money issues stem from stories you've been telling yourself.
- ❖ The Ego does not know the difference between life and death situations and temporary disappointments.
- ❖ God *wants* to give you the tools you need to succeed on your mission. He will never "call" you to do something and then not equip you to succeed.
- ❖ Charge what you're *worth*, based upon the value you bring to the marketplace.
- ❖ Don't just focus on the price of your goods and services. Consider the transformational value of what you bring to the marketplace, and charge accordingly.
- ❖ People will gladly pay for results. If you can give them what they want, you can pretty much write your own check.

TAKE ACTION NOW

1. Take some time to write out your own money beliefs. Fill in the blanks.

   Money is _____.

   When I have money, _____.

   Just completing these two sentences will reveal some of the money blocks keeping you from the abundance you deserve.

2. Commit to doing whatever it takes to busting the money blocks in your life. I've listed a few of my favorite resources in the *Unstoppable Influence Companion Workbook*.

3. Review your current prices. Are you charging what you're worth, given the value your products or services provide? If not, raise your prices!

CHAPTER 19

MONETIZE YOUR MESSAGE

The world will pay you exactly what you bargain for. Your rewards will always be in exact proportion to your service. Do you ask for a lot? If so, you will get a lot. Do you ask for a little? If so, you will get a little.

~ Earl Nightingale

One thing I've heard from some exceptionally gifted individuals over the years is "I can't charge for my gifts because that would be wrong."

Sorry, but I'm calling BS!

Here's the thing—people don't value "free." They may initially act like they do, but they don't. I've offered a handful of scholarships to our programs over the years, and not a *single* scholarship recipient used the program to its potential.

Those who make the biggest financial investments typically get the best results, because they're far more invested not only financially but emotionally and mentally as well.

One friend, after losing 60 pounds in 6 months, offered to share her custom nutrition program with me, so I didn't have to spend money with Cristy. I said, "Hell no! If you give it to me, I won't use it."

When people find value in what you offer, and if they *truly* want it, they'll find the money to buy it. No. Matter. What. Reread that sentence a few times and let it sink in. It's important.

People find the money to buy what's most important to them. Period. So if your audience is unwilling or unable to pay for your products and services, you need to find a new audience. It's really that simple.

When people invest in your products, programs, and services, they're far more likely to invest the time necessary to get the maximum benefit out of them. When they invest time and money, they'll likely achieve results, and that's what it's all about—getting results that will improve people's lives.

For me, it's not about the money. Instead, what we charge is a qualification and commitment mechanism to help our clients get badass results in their businesses and in their lives.

NEGATIVE NANCIES AND NEDS

Fair warning, my fellow Influencer, when you start charging what you're actually worth, you'll need to prepare for the Negative Nancies and Neds, who will be out in full force. The bigger your platform, the greater they are in number.

You'll be able to recognize these Negative Nancies and Neds from a mile away, because they'll be the ones trying to guilt and shame you for charging what you're worth. Ignore them, because they're operating from a different frequency, which is guided 100% by their own Egos. Remember, the Ego is the one that's behind all of your feelings of inadequacy, guilt, anger, shame, blame, worry, anxiety, and the like.

Be compassionate when dealing with Negative Nancies and Neds, but *don't* let them influence you.

I remember a time when we were getting close to wrapping up Day 2 of a 3-day event. This seminar was tremendously valuable, and the organizer had given the audience her very best. By that time, I'd personally received 10 times the price of the ticket in value, and there was another whole day left.

At the end of Day 2, the organizer made an offer to allow a small group of attendees to work with her at a closer level over the next year for between $5,000 and $10,000. The gentleman next to me was appalled. As soon as her presentation was over, he leaned over to me and immediately started bitching.

"How tasteless is she? Trying to sell me something after I paid $500 for this ticket, on *top* of the airfare, hotel, and meals!"

I'm sure he was hoping I'd join his bitch-fest, but instead I asked for permission to share a different perspective. Luckily, this Negative Ned was somewhat intrigued and agreed to listen.

I said, "Some people only want a high school diploma, while others want a college degree, master's, or doctorate, right?"

He agreed.

"Are you angry at colleges and universities for offering undergraduate and graduate programs?"

"Well…no."

"Okay, so if the organizer wants to offer graduate programs for those interested in learning more, why would you get so upset?"

His entire demeanor shifted. It was obvious he'd never thought of it that way.

"To the contrary, if the organizer *didn't* offer the attendees a way to work closely with her to implement what they learned at this event, she would've done them a tremendous disservice."

I continued. "She has the ability to help people achieve their goals. I also happen to know that she invested substantially in her own education to enable her to help others. She deserves to be compensated for her expertise, right?"

The now formerly Negative Ned vigorously agreed, apologized for his previous comments, and thanked me for the new perspective.

The organizer had an obligation not only to offer her services to a hungry audience, but also to charge appropriately for them. So do you. Had the organizer listened to that Negative Ned, I and the others who joined her coaching program wouldn't be where we are today, and you wouldn't be reading this book.

You must be prepared for the detractors, because they're definitely out there. The bigger you get, the more they'll throw virtual stones at you. When that happens, your job is to simply continue doing what you're doing. Charge what you're worth, and don't be ashamed one bit.

In the words of Taylor Swift, "Haters gonna hate, hate, hate…"

Don't allow your light to be dimmed by the naysayers. Stand firmly in your Truth and value. Most of all, remember that not only are you entitled to charge what you're worth, when you do so, you're increasing the likelihood that your clients will get the results they seek.

That's what you want as an Influencer, isn't it? To positively impact people's lives? The way to do that is by helping your clients achieve awesome results. So get out there, charge what you're worth, and change the world.

LET'S REVIEW

- ❖ People rarely value products or services given to them for free.
- ❖ When people find value in what you offer, and if they truly want it, they'll find the money to buy it.
- ❖ If your audience is unwilling or unable to pay for your products and services, find a new audience.
- ❖ The investment you require is a qualification and commitment mechanism to help your clients get awesome results.
- ❖ Be prepared for the detractors because they're out there. The bigger you get, the more they'll throw virtual stones at you. Keep doing what you're doing in spite of the Negative Neds and Nancies. Follow the methodology I've shared with you here, and an enormous

number of positive Pauls and Paulas will overshadow the whiners.

TAKE ACTION NOW

1. Charge what you're worth. Seriously. If that means going to your website right now and increasing your prices, do it. Remember to consider the transformational value of what you bring to your client's life when setting your pricing strategy.

2. Refuse to engage in conversations on social media, email, or otherwise with Negative Neds and Nancies. It's not worth your energy. Focus on the people you *can* serve.

3. Learn more about how to monetize your message at UnstoppableInfluence.com/class.

CHAPTER 20

UNLEASH YOUR INFLUENCE AND AMPLIFY YOUR MESSAGE

The ones who are crazy enough to think they can change the world are the ones who do.

~ Steve Jobs

When it comes to unleashing your message in the world, even the best of the best can't do it alone. Jesus Christ Himself had to have help amplifying His message. He couldn't do it alone.

I can only imagine what would have happened if Jesus had had access to Twitter and Facebook back in the day! But even just using his 12 disciples along with other followers, He was able to spread His message of Good News across the globe.

As an Unstoppable Influencer with a mission uniquely yours, you must do everything possible to maximize the reach of your message. That means embracing concepts or tools that may seem foreign to you or outside your comfort zone. For many, technology (websites, email lists, etc.) is what holds them back from amplifying their message.

"I'm just not good at technology!"

"Technology hates me."

"I can barely turn on a computer or send an email!"

These are just some of the comments I've heard over the years. If they sound familiar, know this—they're stories you've been telling yourself about why you can't use technology to grow your business.

When I hear these excuses, I simply say, "BS."

You don't need to become a programmer or anything like that. I'm not tech-savvy, yet I'm a successful, award-winning internet entrepreneur. You're fully capable of learning the basics and then outsourcing the rest. You don't have to do it all yourself.

TECHNOLOGY IS A TOOL

Technology is one of the single biggest tools that Unstoppable Influencers like you have in your toolbox. A refusal to embrace technology is like saying "Thanks, but no thanks" in response to your purpose.

Technology is a gift from God that enables you to not only connect with other Influencers but to connect with those intended to hear your message. How powerful is that?

To refuse to use this tool because you're technologically challenged is just selfish. It's not your fault, though, for playing victim to technology—it's your Ego's fault. Once you acknowledge that, you can get it under control.

One of my Platinum clients, Anne, was by far my most technology resistant client. She *hated* technology. Her computer would always break down, her emails wouldn't be received, and anything and everything having to do with technology was an absolute nightmare. All this fueled the story concocted by Anne's Ego: "You just can't *do* technology. You're not friends with computers."

Anne told me this story up-front, when she applied to work with us. I told her, as a condition of accepting her into our Platinum mentorship program, she would have to be willing to come to terms with this technology phobia she'd been wrestling with for years.

I said her story that she didn't "do" technology was BS, and that given the extreme amount of talent I saw within her, I wasn't about to let her sit on the sidelines with information that could transform lives around the world.

Fortunately, Anne was highly coachable, so she agreed to rise to the challenge and work on her technology issues for the greater good.

Anne certainly shed her share of tears while wrestling with technology as she brought her message online, but she's grown personally at a rapid rate. She also discovered some of the underlying issues causing her technology blocks—which actually had nothing at all to do with technology.

Anne worked through those blocks and, as a result, technology went from being her foe to being her friend. Best of all, her business started growing rapidly as a result of her decision to embrace technology instead of resisting it.

Instead of working with only a couple of people per month, she began working with dozens, and she was just getting started.

To automate and systematize your message so you can make a big impact, you must embrace technology.

If that concept freaks you out, then you must commit, like Anne did, to uncovering the source of that resistance and bust through, so that you're positioned to embrace technology and use it to the fullest extent possible.

HOW TO AUTOMATE AND SYSTEMATIZE YOUR MESSAGE

The tools available to automate and systematize your message are endless. Because they change rapidly, I'll only discuss them in general. In the *Unstoppable Influence Companion Workbook*, you'll find a list of some of our current favorite tools for automating and systematizing our business.

WEBSITE

Your website is the cornerstone of sharing your message with the world. This is a centralized place where your followers and prospective clients can learn more about you and your business.

Your website is available 24 hours a day, 7 days a week, rain or shine, snow, sleet, or hail. It enables people to connect with you even when you're asleep, working with others, or on vacation.

It also allows people to get to know you at their own pace. Some people are immersive types—they'll dive into every nook and cranny of your website on the first visit. Others will "check you out" off and on for weeks or months. One client followed me online for *two years* before making a purchase.

Depending on what you're offering your audience, it may be a good idea to include a blog on your website. A blog, or web log, is like a digital newspaper; it's simply a series of articles or videos. You can see an example at NatashaHazlett.com.

Your website, at a minimum, should include the following:

- **About** page that tells more about you and your company
- **Contact** page that provides your contact details
- An offer or free gift to join your **email list**
- Opportunities for people to **purchase** your goods or services
- **Social media** buttons
- **Testimonials/reviews** (if applicable)

SOCIAL MEDIA

Love it or hate it, social media is here to stay. Currently, Facebook, YouTube, Instagram, Twitter, LinkedIn, and Pinterest are the giants, but this area is constantly evolving.

Social media offers the opportunity to quickly and easily connect with and get to know people around the world. People can "follow" you and your business and make comments on your posts using words, pictures, or videos.

Plus, your message could go viral, which is defined as reaching five million people within one week. Can you imagine the impact you could make if *your* message went viral? It can happen—and when it does, it can transform lives.

One of my favorite viral examples is the 2014 ALS Ice Bucket Challenge. Its origin is debated, but here's how it worked. People were challenged to either record themselves getting a bucket of ice water dumped on their heads or to make a donation to the ALS Association (and many did both) to fund research for Amyotrophic Lateral Sclerosis, is a progressive neurodegenerative disease. On the video, the participant challenged three additional people to complete the Ice Bucket Challenge and post their videos on Facebook.

The challenge went viral and was so popular that celebrities and political figures hopped on board—including President George W. Bush, Bill Gates, Matt Lauer, and basketball legend, LeBron James. Ultimately, the ALS Ice Bucket Challenge was completed by an estimated 2.4 million people and raised $115 million for ALS Research, all in a matter of weeks.

This, my friend, is the power of social media. The great part is, you don't need your post to go viral to make a massive impact in people's lives. I've had countless people message me after one of my Facebook Lives to tell me how my video changed their lives.

For example, as a result of my decision to open up and share my weight-loss journey, I had over 50 friends commit to eating real food by following the Code Red Lifestyle. Some got rid of the "baby weight" that had them feeling self-conscious, while others were able to escape the fog of depression and take their lives back. All of them were inspired by my vulnerable story, which I shared with the world on social media.

That's just one example of the power of this tool. The reason I began working with Cristy in the first place was because I followed her on Facebook and watched her videos.

Likewise, the reason Cristy started working with me is because she saw my videos, website, and testimonials and wanted me to help her grow her business.

Social media is a powerful tool that you *must* embrace as an Unstoppable Influencer.

Whenever I suggest that people use social media, I typically get two objections.

Objection #1. There are too many social media platforms. I don't have time to learn them all.

My Response: Me neither! You don't need to learn or participate on all the platforms. The key is to understand which platforms your audience uses, pick one, and learn the basics. Once you feel comfortable with that one, you can move on to the next.

You can also use social media automation tools to streamline your content across multiple social media channels with the click of a button. I've listed those resources for you in the *Unstoppable Influence Companion Workbook*.

Objection #2. I'm a private person, so I don't want to share on social media (or I hate the way I look on camera).

My Response: I get it. This objection kept me from posting anything consistent or meaningful on Facebook for *years*.

It wasn't until I got a swift kick in the ass from my friend Heather, a social media ninja, that I started viewing Facebook in a totally different light. Here's what I learned.

Social media is the ultimate connection and leadership tool, where people can get to know, like, and trust you. It's a way to easily empower, inspire, and impact thousands or even millions of lives.

By staying off social media (like I did for years), you're depriving the world of your light and your message.

If you can't stand people who share obnoxious "Send this to five people or you'll die" posts, then don't share them. If you hate seeing pictures of people's meals because you think they're oversharing, then don't post pictures of your own food. If political posts piss you off, don't write or share them yourself.

You do *you* on social media.

A REALITY CHECK

I told everyone that the reason I hated social media, and Facebook specifically, was for privacy reasons and that I didn't want to overshare. But that wasn't the real reason.

In reality, I wasn't posting on Facebook because I was ashamed of my appearance, and I was afraid people would judge me. I was also terrified that people would disapprove of what I was talking about, or that they'd think my message was foolish.

My approval addiction had reared its ugly head once again and was actively sabotaging my mission. Once I acknowledged this, the Unstoppable Influencer in me said, "Okay, all those stories about Facebook are nonsense. Toss 'em and let's start changing lives!"

In that moment, I committed to sharing my Truth on social media. August 1, 2016, was the first day I went live on Facebook, and it felt great. You can see my video at UnstoppableInfluence.com/firstlive.

People have told me that their lives have been transformed from my videos, and the same can happen for you if you will embrace social media as a tool to expand your sphere of influence

You don't need to be anyone other than yourself. And don't worry for one second about trying to be "perfect." Remember, it's when you're *imperfect* that people connect with you even more.

Here's an embarrassing but true example. When I first moved to Idaho, Rich asked me to shoot a video introducing people to a free training. It was my first video and I was *horrible*. I was squinting, the editing was choppy, and I looked so damn uncomfortable (because I *was!*).

We put the video on my blog, but I secretly hoped no one would see it, because it was *that* bad.

A month later, Rich decided to start advertising on YouTube. He asked me to shoot a new video that he could use for an ad. Because I hated being on camera, and because my previous video had sucked, I ignored his request.

Since Rich knew that the chances of me doing another video anytime soon was slim to none, he grabbed the video from my blog and ran an ad with it.

That one horrendous video has racked up over 105,000 views and resulted in tens of thousands of people starting to follow us, not to mention hundreds of thousands of dollars in revenue.

I can't tell you the number of people who said that painfully awkward video of me in the river is the reason they wanted to do business with us. In fact, that imperfect video ended up being the foundation of our entire business.

So don't let your desire to be "perfect" hold you back, because it's the imperfection and authenticity that people crave. If you want to watch the video that started it all, go to Unstoppable-Influence.com/firstvideo.

Hopefully by now you're open to embracing social media, or at a minimum, willing to do the work necessary to remove any blocks causing your resistance. The world is waiting to hear from you—don't keep them waiting long!

EMAIL AUTO-RESPONDER

If you're going to spread your influence in the world, and you want to have a consistent presence in your followers' lives, you must connect with them via email.

Obviously, it's impractical for you (or your staff) to individually email people on a regular basis. You'll need a quick and easy method of disseminating your messages.

Enter the fabulous auto-responder. An auto-responder is a tool that allows people to enter their contact information into a web form and sign up to receive content, training, or specials from you.

An auto-responder enables you to communicate with your list of clients and prospective clients. With it, you can contact hundreds, thousands, even millions of people by writing an email and then sending it out to your entire email database with one click.

If you've been through any internet-marketing training, you've likely heard that the money is "in your list." That's true—sort of. The money doesn't actually come from your list; it comes from the *relationships you build* with the people on your list.

Far too many business owners have no automated way to stay in touch with their clients or prospective clients. Or if they have an auto-responder, they rarely use it, because they're afraid to "annoy" their fans. As an Unstoppable Influencer, you have a moral obligation to be "top of mind" in your fans' lives.

To do this, you can't simply hope that people love your website so much that they'll remember you forever. In today's hectic world, that won't happen.

Plus, you don't own your social media profile—the big companies like Facebook and Google do. They permit you to use their platform, but have the right to revoke that permission and delete your profile at any time. So it's critical that you have a list that you *own*.

To recap, the tool that helps you create your list, capture the interest of prospective buyers, and build a relationship with them on autopilot so they can get to know, like, and trust you is an auto-responder.

There are numerous auto-responders available. I've listed our tried-and-true favorites in the *Unstoppable Influence Companion Workbook*.

Once you have an auto-responder, you need to link it to your website and social media profiles so they'll work seamlessly together. You don't need to know how to do this yourself; you can find someone to assist you. In the *Unstoppable Influence Companion Workbook*, I've included a few of my favorite resources for outsourcing techy tasks. If you still haven't downloaded your copy of the workbook, get it now for FREE at UnstoppableInfluence.com/gift.

AUTOMATED MARKETING AND SALES FUNNEL

Last but not least, to truly amplify your message and systematize your business so you can make SWISS dollars, you'll need an automated marketing and sales funnel. This is a non-negotiable must-have for every single Unstoppable Influencer with a business, because you can serve people around the world 24 hours a day, 7 days a week.

A funnel integrates with your auto-responder and allows people to get to know, like, and trust you, learn about what you have to offer, and then buy your products and services.

Some software is so snazzy it'll connect not only your auto-responder and sales pages, but will also process payments and deliver content to your buyers. How cool is that?

Several options are available for marketing and sales funnel automation. I've listed our personal favorite in the *Unstoppable Influence Companion Workbook*.

The one objection I frequently get when I'm helping an entrepreneur design their automated funnel is "I don't want to be a pushy or cheesy salesperson."

Here's my take on that: You're the head honcho of your marketing and sales machine. If you don't want to be pushy or cheesy, then don't be. That said, you still have an obligation to sell. Without fail, when I tell my clients that, they look at me like a deer in headlights.

"But Natasha, I don't *like* to sell! I don't want people to think badly of me."

Look, this business of "I don't like selling" is another one of the Ego's patented BS stories that keeps awesome people like you on the sidelines, preventing you from making an impact.

Let's bust that myth right now. Are you ready?

REJECTION, SHMAJECTION

First, the *real* reason your Ego has made that story up is that you likely tried to sell something in the past, like Girl Scout cookies when you were little, and someone said, "No thank you" or "I'm not interested."

That hurt your feelings. You felt rejected. Feeling rejected sucks. Your Ego doesn't want you to feel sucky, so it concocts a story about selling and voilà, your fear of sales was born.

The reality is that someone saying "No thank you" has absolutely nothing to do with you. They just didn't want the cookies. That's it. Not everyone wants what you have to sell, and that's okay.

When someone says no to your offer, it's typically because it's not the right *time* for them, or they may not resonate with your message or style. That's okay. Don't take it personally.

As world-renowned sales expert Don Hutson says:

> Nobody sells everyone and nobody can miss them all either! Everyone has conversion rates between 1% and 99%. The key is to monitor yours, and constantly remind yourself that you must improve it. Once you have internalized that mandate, you'll improve.

By the way, with an automated marketing and sales funnel, you'll never face rejection. The funnel does the prospecting and closing for you, plus it bears the burden of rejection. How sweet is that?

That said, you still have an obligation to sell. Why? You're an Unstoppable Influencer. Part of our Manifesto reads:

> We use our influence for good. We know our worth and charge accordingly.

If you're using your influence for *good*, and your products and services make a positive impact in people's lives, then you have an obligation to share them. Period.

Likewise, you have an obligation to charge what you're worth. Remember, people rarely value items that are free. There's a reason they call it a "buy-in." The exchange of money for a good or service creates an internal connection, which increases the likelihood the buyer will take the necessary action to use their purchase, thereby getting the intended result.

Of course, this isn't *always* the case, but for the most part, it is. *If* by chance they don't achieve the intended results, it's almost always because they used their "free will" to avoid taking a necessary action.

I'll use Cristy as an example. Her nutrition program has transformed lives, including mine. I've had phenomenal results just by following what she told me to do. I have friends who also hired her and got their own nutrition programs. They lost some weight, but then quickly gained it back. Was that Cristy's fault?

Hell no! I'm living proof that if people follow what she says, they'll lose weight and keep it off. But some people aren't ready to dump the pounds for good.

The same thing happens in our business. We have a proven formula that helps people boost their income and level of influence without working longer hours. We know it works, because Cristy, Heather, Michael, Cynthia, and others are living proof. However, not everyone that comes to us is ready to take action on what we teach. That's their choice—free will, baby!

The moral of the story is you can't sit on the sidelines not selling your product because you're worried people may say "no thank you" or believe that what you sell "doesn't work." If you know it works, you *have* to sell it—no matter what.

You're not responsible for people's inaction. That's on them, not you.

I remember when Cristy was worried about scaling up her business. She thought that without her one-on-one hand-holding, people wouldn't succeed. Plus, she confided in me that there were several clients she didn't want to work with because she didn't think they'd "stick with the program," and Cristy only wanted success stories.

I asked, "So what if they choose to disregard your advice?"

Out popped Cristy's sneaky Ego. "Well, I'll look like a failure, like my program doesn't work. Then other people won't want to buy it."

I asked, "Is that true? That your program doesn't work, just because one person doesn't follow it?"

"No."

"Have other people gained back their weight?"

"Yes."

"Did that impact your business? Did you stop selling programs?"

"No."

"Do you have success stories of people who have lost the weight?"

"Yes."

"So you won't be a failure if this one person doesn't succeed, right?"

"I guess you're right."

As it turns out, Cristy's original fear—that she'd look like a failure and that others would think her program didn't work and wouldn't buy it—was just a BS story.

YOUR JOB: PLANTING SEEDS

I used that moment to teach Cristy the concept of planting seeds in her business. This is a critical lesson for you too, as an Unstoppable Influencer.

As Influencers, we'll spend our lives planting seeds. Not every seed you plant will bloom under your watch. Sometimes a seed takes longer to bloom or requires another gardener to tend to it. That particular gardener's care is what was needed for that seed to bloom. Then there are times that someone else has planted a seed, and your care is what's needed for it to bloom.

I explained to Cristy that by working with people in her Code Red program, she was frequently planting the first seed of healthy eating and a sustainable way to lose weight. Sometimes people aren't ready to "bloom" and lose the weight at that moment. But months or years later, they may come back, or they may take what they learned from Cristy and finally drop the weight. When that happens, she has *still* made a positive impact in their life. That's what matters.

Likewise, in our business, we've helped tens of thousands of entrepreneurs from around the world. Some have been through our training and coaching programs and have taken that information and gone on to become extremely successful.

Others have come to us after working with another business or marketing coach, and start to thrive. Perhaps it was the right time, or maybe our "style"— regardless, we helped them bloom.

Either way, I know that we're operating in alignment with our purpose—to plant seeds within entrepreneurs that will enable them to get the clarity, confidence, and strategies they need to boost their income and influence in the world without working longer hours.

Sometimes we get to see the seed bloom and sometimes we don't. Although the results-oriented Ego of mine wants to see every seed bloom, in my heart I know that I'm doing the work I'm intended to do.

So remember, you may not get to see every seed bloom. Plant them anyway.

GET OUT THERE AND SELL!

When you sell your products and services, you'll be helping people attain the results they desire, and that's a great thing. *Plus,* you'll be earning money, which will expand your sphere of influence and enable you to serve even *more.* How awesome is that?

Don Hutson reminded me:

> The negative image of selling that still lingers
> in the minds of some people is an old story that
> no longer has merit. Selling is NOT pushing

something onto people that they don't want or need. That is manipulation of the worst order. In today's world, there are few places for those folks to hide! Today, selling is all about helping people reach their goals by providing for them the tools, ideas, and counsel to help them.

He then advised me to "erase the old stories and get out there and help people get what they want!"

These words hit home in a big way. Realizing that selling my products and services allows me to help others and ultimately fulfill my mission radically transformed my view about selling. I'm no longer afraid to sell. In fact, I embrace the opportunity.

Selling, especially through an automated sales and marketing funnel, is the fourth and final tech tool you'll need in your toolbox as an Unstoppable Influencer.

I wish it were more complicated than that (actually, I don't), but it's not. With the help of technology, your job as an Unstoppable Influencer is easier than ever. You just need to equip yourself with these tools and use them to change the world.

LET'S REVIEW

- ✧ When it comes to amplifying your message, even the very best can't do it alone.
- ✧ As an Unstoppable Influencer, you must do everything in your power to maximize the reach of your message, even if that means stepping outside your comfort zone.
- ✧ Your Ego is one badass storyteller. Recognize the difference between BS stories and the Truth when it comes to amplifying your message.

- As an Unstoppable Influencer, you must embrace technology as a necessary tool to amplify your message.
- The four technology tools of an Unstoppable Influencer are:
  - ✓ A website
  - ✓ Social media
  - ✓ Email auto-responder
  - ✓ Automated marketing and sales funnel

  Collectively, they can change the game for you!
- Your duty is to plant seeds. Even if they don't bloom on your watch, plant them anyway.

TAKE ACTION NOW

1. Make a list of the stories you've told yourself about the four tech tools discussed in this chapter. For each story, decide whether it's true or false. If the story is false, create a new story to take its place.

2. Commit to a launch date for your automated sales and marketing funnel, if applicable. Write down the date and sign your name by it. Then do whatever is necessary to complete your funnel.

3. In your journal or *Unstoppable Influence Companion Workbook*, write down how your products and/or services can change people's lives. Whenever you are nervous to sell, reread what you wrote to remind yourself how you are helping your clients succeed.

CONCLUSION

You must be the change you wish to see in the world.

-- Gandhi

When I sat down to write this book, I had no idea what I'd write about. I only knew two things.

1. I trusted that God would provide the inspiration.
2. My words would inspire people to find the light within and share it with the world.

I didn't know how to weave my experiences into a roadmap for others on the journey of Unstoppable Influence—but God did.

If there's one thing I hope you'll take from this book, in addition to knowing you've been tapped as an Unstoppable Influencer, it's this: To unleash your influence in the world for the greatest good, you *must* connect regularly with your Source.

Writing has allowed me to consistently connect with God in a way I've never experienced. The level of joy, peace, and satisfaction I've felt operating in-Spirit during this time is unparalleled. I want to feel this way every single day, and I'm committed to making it my reality.

The process of writing my first book has been a humbling exercise that has strengthened my faith muscle like no other. I didn't have all the answers before I began, but I started anyway.

Although my mentors have sent me stacks of materials about how to write a book, they've remained untouched.

Instead, I chose to let my soul guide me, and I embraced the unknown. I danced out of my comfort zone. To keep myself accountable, I told my Facebook followers that I was writing this book and gave them regular updates. Their excitement and support throughout the writing process was the extra fuel I needed on some days. Thanks, y'all! (You know who you are.)

Truth be told, as I typed this page, I wasn't 100% certain how to turn my manuscript into an actual book. Yet I had complete confidence that just as God had blessed me with the inspiration necessary to complete it, He would pave the way for it to get into the hands of the people who need it.

My experience writing this book is similar to your journey as an Unstoppable Influencer. You won't have all the answers at first. You must get started before you're ready. You'll have to step out of your comfort zone, tackle fear and doubt like a boss, and trust in the ability of your higher power to guide you to the fulfillment of your purpose.

Looking back, by turning my focus away from ME and redirecting it toward God, I reconnected with my light, even when everything else seemed dark. This journey enabled my light to grow, and it has also enabled me to light the path for other Influencers around the world.

The seed of Unstoppable Influence has been planted within you now. I hope I'll have the opportunity to meet you in person one day. I can't wait to hear about your calling and how you've unleashed your influence in the world.

In the words of Psalm 20:4: "May He give you the desire of your heart and make all of your plans succeed." (NIV)

Remember, you're here *on* purpose and *for* a purpose. You're not alone on your journey, because you have the benefit of your Creator's infinite knowledge and a community of fellow Unstoppable Influencers who are here to support you along the way.

If you've made it here, let's do a happy dance together and say it with me…

THE END

But not really. You and I both know this is *just* the beginning!

P.S. Can I even add a P.S. to a book? Looks like I just did. If you haven't joined our Unstoppable Influence Community, what are you waiting for?

Go to UnstoppableInfluence.com/group and let's connect!

ENDNOTES

1. Brown, Les. *Expert Industry Association Annual Conference.* San Diego, September 2013.

2. Rev. 1:8 KJV.

3. Miller, Dan. *48 Days to the Work You Love.* B&H Publishing Group, Nashville, 2010.

4. Sincero, Jen. *You Are a Badass.* Running Press, Philadelphia, 2013.

5. The Emotion Code™ was created by Dr. Bradley Nelson. The theory behind The Emotion Code™ is that emotionally-charged events from your past can still be haunting you in the form of "trapped emotions," emotional energies that literally inhabit your body. Trapped emotions can create pain, emotional stress, and eventual disease. With a skilled Emotion Code practitioner, you can quickly and easily rid yourself of damaging emotional baggage and "trapped emotions," and find and tear down your "Heart-wall" to unlock better health, relationships, and abundance. Learn more at: http://www.drbradleynelson.com/the-emotion-code/

6. Bachinsky, Anna. "When God Makes Us Wait," The Praying Woman. Accessed August 29, 2017. http://theprayingwoman.com/when-god-makes-you-wait/.

7. Christopher, Eric. "Marcus Lemonis: The Man, The Myth, The Marriage Counselor" June 8, 2016. http://www.huffingtonpost.com/eric-e-rock-christopher/marcus-lemonis-the-man-th_b_10341916.html, Last Accessed September 12, 2017.

8. Marcus Lemonis. https://www.marcuslemonis.com/pages/about-us

YOU'RE INVITED!

It's time to get FIRED UP, re-ignite your flame and make the world even brighter!

You can get the clarity, confidence and strategies you need to unleash your influence in a BIG way this year while *finally* getting paid what you're worth...

I've created challenges, a home study course and coaching programs to help Influencers just like you who are ready to step out of their comfort zone and step up their game!

As Mary Morrissey says, "inspiration without action is merely entertainment." So it's important that you take the necessary steps to put what you've just learned into action.

I would be honored to help you!

Learn more about the programs I'm currently offering at: UnstoppableInfluence.com/programs

I look forward to the opportunity to connect with you and see how you're sharing your light with the world! Email me at natasha@UnstoppableInfluence.com and tell me how you're using this book to make a difference!

With Love,
Natasha

ACKNOWLEDGEMENTS

To my parents, George and Nayla Nassar, and my brother, George III, for always believing in me and supporting my "unconventional" journey.

To Russell Brunson, thank you for your unwavering belief in me and your support over the years. I would not be here without you.

To Cristy Nickel, you helped me take my life back, and for that I will be forever grateful.

To Emma Tiebens, the epitome of an Unstoppable Influencer, who has continued to inspire me throughout her courageous battle with cancer.

To Julie Ann Eason, thank you for gently nudging me for two years to "write the damn book" and for your Non-Fiction Book Academy. It has been an integral part of my journey to publish my first book.

To Don Hutson and Terri Murphy, thank you for the final kick in the pants to get my book completed this year. I did it!

To Julia Willson, thanks for helping make this book better (and far more grammatically correct).

To Carol Lamoreaux, Mandy Keene, Angela Hoover, Melissa Walsh, Jessica Tookey, Estelle Winsett, Joan Biddle, and Joy Ruffle for your help with this book.

To Michele Gleason, my friend and soul mentor, for allowing me to use your gorgeous zen den to write this book and for supporting my journey!

To Ann Sieg, thank you for believing in me in the early days and giving me a platform to find and share my voice and message.

To my amazing clients, you know who you are, thank you for your loving support and encouragement. You inspire me with your passion to transform lives, and I am honored to be on the journey with such Unstoppable Influencers. Y'all are the originals!

ABOUT THE AUTHOR

Natasha Nassar Hazlett is best known as a Personal Brand Strategist. She empowers entrepreneurs around the world with the clarity, confidence, and strategies they need to boost their income and influence while working less, by monetizing their message online.

In addition to being a mentor and coach, Natasha is a speaker, award-winning internet marketer, practicing attorney, and the co-founder of Fast Forward Marketing, LLC with her husband Rich. Most importantly, though, she's mom to an adorable little girl.

The *Idaho Business Review* honored Natasha with their 2013 Idaho Women of the Year award, and she has been honored multiple times with the Rising Star Award by *Super Lawyers* magazine.

You can learn more about Natasha at: NatashaHazlett.com and connect with her on social media at:

Facebook: NatashaHazlett.com/FB

Instagram: NatashaHazlett.com/IG

YouTube: NatashaHazlett.com/YT

PUBLISHING

Cover credit: Eled Cernik; artwork created by Stacey Hill Design; author photo by Erin Blackwell Studio

Quantity sales. Special discounts are available on quantity purchases by corporations, associations, and others. For details, contact Fast Forward Marketing LLC at 6126 W. State Street, Suite 605, Boise, Idaho, 83714, support@unstoppableinfluence.com

84126410R10149

Made in the USA
Middletown, DE
17 August 2018